Lions And Cows Dining Together

And 111 Other Sermon Ideas

Terry Cain

CSS Publishing Company, Inc., Lima, Ohio

LIONS AND COWS DINING TOGETHER

Copyright © 2005 by
CSS Publishing Company, Inc.
Lima, Ohio

The original purchaser may photocopy material in this publication for use as it was intended (i.e., worship material for worship use; educational material for classroom use; dramatic material for staging or production). No additional permission is required from the publisher for such copying by the original purchaser only. Inquiries should be addressed to: Permissions, CSS Publishing Company, Inc., P.O. Box 4503, Lima, Ohio 45802-4503.

Library of Congress Cataloging-in-Publication Data

Cain, Terry, 1938-
  Lions and cows dining together : and 111 other sermon ideas / Terry Cain.
      p. cm.
  Includes index.
  ISBN 0-7880-2339-X (alk. paper)
  1. Sermons—Outlines, syllabi, etc. I. Title.

BV4223.C285 2004
251'.02—dc22

2004023797

For more information about CSS Publishing Company resources, visit our website at www.csspub.com or e-mail us at custserv@csspub.com or call (800) 241-4056.

Cover design by Chris Patton
ISBN 0-7880-2339-X

PRINTED IN U.S.A.

This book is dedicated to my family:

My late father, Harold Cain
My late mother, Dorothy Cain
My wife, Sue Cain
My son, Terry Cain
My daughter, Sherry Clements
My son-in-law, Dan Clements

Acknowledgments

My special thanks to friend and colleague, Jerry McInnis, a retired United Methodist minister and to my wife, Susie, who were able to salvage this manuscript enough to make it readable!

Table Of Contents

Introduction   9

P.
1. What's The Point Of Living?   15
2. Did Jesus Really Yell At A Tree?   16
3. Plays Well With Others: B+   18
4. Let Me Tell You What You Believe   20
5. No Yellow Flags!   21
6. God Always Wins At Hide And Seek   23
7. Should Acolytes Wear Sneakers?   25
8. Mom, Where Did We Come From?   27
9. One Bible — So Many Churches!   28
10. Guns Яn't Us   30

Q.
1. Ate With Any Wicked People Lately?   33
2. When Your Friends Are Naughty   35
3. Love Your Neighbor — Very Carefully!   37
4. Worship Is More Than Just Staying Awake   39
5. Little Orphan Annie Complex   41
6. Would Jesus Stretch The Truth?   43
7. A Sunday School For Adults Only!   44
8. Up Close And Personal   46
9. There Are No Holy Wars   48
10. Pink Bunny Batteries   51

R.
1. My God Doesn't Make Tornadoes   55
2. In The Name Of God!   57
3. An Unidentified Naked Male Running From The Scene   59
4. Can You Be Trusted With Crayons And Scissors?   61
5. Is It Time To Modernize The Gospel?   62
6. The Day That God Changed His Mind   64

7.	Touch Me, Turn Me On, And Burn Me Down	66
8.	Becoming A Tricky Old Dog	68
9.	How Vulgar Can We Be?	70
10.	When Christianity Becomes A Waste Of Time	72

S.

1.	When Worlds Collide: Sacred And Secular	75
2.	Imagine That!	77
3.	You Thought It Couldn't Get Any Worse	78
4.	Some Things You Don't Want To Know	80
5.	Lions And Cows Dining Together: Seeing Is Believing	82
6.	Analysis Of A Saloon	84
7.	Get Over It!	87
8.	Three Little Pigs — Jesus' Version	89
9.	Can Pagan Objects Be Sanitized?	90
10.	A Just-In-Case Arrangement With God	93

T.

1.	Rainbow-colored Coats And Green-eyed Monsters	95
2.	A Buddhist, A Mormon, And An Atheist Were Out In A Boat Fishing	97
3.	A Blueprint For Dying	99
4.	Developing Extra-Ray Vision	101
5.	Paul Said The Darnedest Things	104
6.	Does The Sneaky Side Of Us Enjoy Violence?	106
7.	When Religion Turns Into A Circus	108
8.	You *Can* Learn To Like Spinach, Liver, And Theology	111
9.	A Bodyguard Named Jesus	113
10.	From Inside A Really Big Empty	115

U.

1.	Watch Those Promises!	117
2.	Is The Bible Racist?	119
3.	The Four Most Beautiful Things God Ever Created	120
4.	Did The Wise Men Sleep In The Stable?	123

5. When Kids Go Bad	125
6. Methinks Thou Dost Not Protest Too Much	126
7. Noah And The Ark And Other True Stories	128
8. Putting Leftovers In The Offering Plate	131
9. Do You Ever Pretend To Be A Christian?	133
10. Our Cat Doesn't Know We Don't Have A Cat	135

V.

1. "Feel Good" Religion: A Contemporary Theology	137
2. Take This Religion Test	139
3. Could Uncle Tom Be A Christ Figure?	140
4. Knowing What To Know	142
5. God Needs An Alias	143
6. It's The Least You Can Do	145
7. Who Do You Love Better: God Or Me?	147
8. The Ubiquitous Nature Of Religion	149
9. Catch Me If You Can	150
10. Hell: But, It's A Dry Heat	152

W.

1. Finding Your Way From Nazareth To Jerusalem	155
2. Preaching To The Choir	155
3. Should The Universe Make Sense — And Why?	157
4. Neither Peacock Nor Worm	159
5. Will Reverend Tortoise Ever Catch Doctor Hare?	161
6. It's Time To Quit	163
7. Have You Hugged Your God Today?	165
8. Religion That Will Scare You To Death	166
9. Drive-Thru-Window Church	168
10. Life's Most Pressing Question	170

X.

1. Why Hasn't Jesus Offended You?	173
2. If It Isn't In The Bible, It Should Be	175
3. Reasons Not To Go To Church	177
4. Religion In A Disposable Culture	178
5. Too Heavenly Minded To Be Any Earthly Good	180

6.	Pearly Gates Entrance Exam	182
7.	Can Compassion Be Turned On Like A Faucet?	184
8.	I Embarrassed God Again Yesterday	186
9.	Why In The World Is There A World?	187
10.	Should You Be Sophisticated Or Naive?	189

Y.
1.	What If Your Minister Misleads You?	191
2.	Will Sports Craziness Infiltrate The Church?	192
3.	Batman, Wonder Woman, Jesus, And Other Superheroes	194
4.	How Do You Define Yourself?	196
5.	Everything I Needed To Know I Learned In Sunday School	198
6.	So You Think You Got Away With It	200
7.	Do Circumstances Ever Justify A Sin?	202
8.	Goldilocks And The Three Bears Problem	204
9.	What Did He Do That Was So Bad?	206
10.	Don't I Look Nice?	208

Z.
1.	Knock, Knock — Who's There?	211
2.	The Multi-Billion-Dollar Rodent Den	213
3.	Wicked, But Worth It	215
4.	Pilgrim Or Tourist?	217
5.	Blemishes And Biblical Authentication	219
6.	A Dangerous Way To Read Your Bible	221
7.	Skeletons In The Church Closet	223
8.	The Christian And False Besmirchment	224
9.	We Need To Talk	226
10.	If You Can't Say Something Nice ...	227

Bonus Sermons
1.	Let Me Tell You How To Vote	231
2.	Oh, One More Thing	234

Subject Or Topic Index	237

Introduction

As I was saying ... (This is a companion volume to a book titled, *Shaking Wolves Out Of Cherry Trees*, and consequently is designed to pick up where that book left off, with sections P through Z). This is a book of sermon ideas with, hopefully, catchy titles. Each sermon has a purpose statement, which is only intended to identify the focus of the message. It is not intended to be the purpose statement in which the speaker tries to set the specific goal for the message. That is left to the speaker's ingenuity. The purpose statement is followed in each case with some discussion concerning the topic, usually some possible "points" for an outline, some scripture suggestions, and perhaps on occasion an illustration, or humor. These are intended to be "pump primers" with the speaker filling in the etceteras. While many philosophic pieces, editorials, essays, and so forth offer you and me dogmatic opinions; these message ideas are only meant to point down the trail as you develop your own theological presentations. Even the titles found here are only signposts to general directions. You will undoubtedly create better ones.

As I visit many other churches in eager anticipation of hearing exciting sermons, my biggest criticism would be that the messages are nearly all the same. I believe some homiletics professor once said there is only one message with different titles and illustrations. That message seems to be, "Get right with God," or one of its many variations: "Believe in Jesus and be saved," "We need a strong faith in God and Jesus," and so forth. I strongly disagree with such a narrow focus. There are so many serious theological ideas and needs of persons that should command attention. Seldom — very seldom — do I hear a message addressing one of life's critical questions or issues that I hope are covered by the messages in these two books. One of my serious goals with these sermon starters is to be as comprehensive as possible. I tried to cover all the bases so that the reader should find a wide and inclusive variety of topics.

Related to this last thought, we preachers rarely examine such vital social issues such as racism, war, gun control, sex, capital punishment, and the like. I feel very strongly that *the teachings of Jesus are especially relevant* to all serious concerns of this nature and we must make definitive statements on the Christian's responsibilities regarding these subjects. If we only "preach the love of Jesus" and expect every member to translate that into social action, we will be dismal failures in making any impact on social concerns. This is exactly what happened in the days of slavery. Christians by the millions were told all about the love of Jesus and it did nothing to eradicate slavery. We must be specific and direct. Because we are straying into dangerous waters, please read the section on "controversial preaching" in the introduction of the first book.

Who Is It Intended For?

Everyone! Laypersons and clergy alike may find this book helpful as ideas and titles for their sermons or talks given to groups (women's, men's, youth, and so forth). It can be used for personal devotions. It can be read as a series of religious issues or theological ideas for meditation, criticism, analysis, or starters. If sermons are really helpful for us to hear and think about, then these could be treated as mini-sermons.

While this book is intended for pastors to jump-start sermons or just trigger some interesting thinking (consider it a "do-it-yourself" kit), conceivably many of these messages deal with provocative subjects and, regardless of whether they are right or wrong, could be used by small groups of pastors to discuss "if," and how, they should be preached. If the theology strikes anyone as unpalatable, it still does us all good to struggle with opposing points of view. A mature person benefits from reading the arguments on both sides of the issue.

Finally, homiletics professors in most of the seminaries across the country will probably choose to use this book as one of their texts. Where else will they find gathered together under one cover, so many fine examples of the complete variety of "what *not* to do" when preparing sermons?

Preaching Gets Complicated

Life is complicated. Ideas are complicated. It doesn't take long into a career of preaching to find out how difficult these complications make preaching. You start with what seemed a simple idea only to find yourself over your head for one of several reasons. You may venture into an area with no easy answers. You may be startled by a seemingly irresolvable contradiction. The subject chosen may be too rich and narrowing the focus is too taxing. Your subject may be unpreachable, either because it strikes too close to home for a select few in the congregation as to make it appear that they have been singled out over all the others, or because there is no easy way to proceed to clarify the issue.

Struggling through the labyrinth of ideas in a sermon, we stumble upon a seeming contradiction. For example, in a sermon such as, Z-1, "Knock, Knock — Who's There?" our subject is how to defend ourselves from the aggressive zealot who assaults us on our doorstep claiming the faith they are offering us is so much better than our own. As we prepare this sermon, it dawns on us the unwanted visitor at our door may be offering us God's Word, and we may be guilty of undermining that message such as in sermon G-5, "Stop Putting Out God's Fires." Should we make reference to this contradiction and take the time to deal with it now or in a later sermon? Resolving the perplexities of important ideas is not an easy task.

Closely related to this discussion is the problem of keeping our messages concise and short enough to be tolerable for our congregations. Seldom do you or I preach such riveting sermons that church members are entranced in such rapt attention as to not notice how long our message is. The trouble is that we should spend adequate time in preparation to sharpen and focus our ideas. Consequently, as we go over and over the sermon, we find ourselves adding new, and seemingly indispensable, material. Going over the sermon to sharpen and focus our thoughts is not the time to lengthen and expand, although the temptation is close to uncontrollable. We feel what we have to say is so important and so good, it can't possibly be left out. Not very often do we achieve a message that is short and at the same time poignant and stunning. Yet when we are able to pair down by sharpening our focus, it often enhances the clarity.

Preacher As King Or Queen

In the first volume I mentioned the ostentatious nature of preaching. I believe there is a danger related to this phenomenon: a possible tendency for some of us preacher types to suffer from ego extension. The nature of preaching itself — wearing a robe and stole, standing behind a pulpit or elevated on a chancel area, and proclaiming the Word of God — is awesome when we contemplate it. There has been a concerted effort for preachers to "get out from behind the pulpit" so as not to "put barriers between them and the people," which may not really make that much difference. Other aspects of our ministry such as administering the communion elements, baptizing, marrying, and burying people, may carry over into our preaching posture. As keepers and interpreters of the truth, we get to expound on how everyone should live and speak. Unless we are careful, we can assume the role of king or queen. Even some of the old time chancel chairs resembled thrones. It behooves us to be on guard concerning our preaching preparation and delivery. Have we sometimes accepted the role of reigning monarch — perhaps unawares? Can we recognize it in ourselves if it happens?

The tendency for some pastors to become controlling, manipulating, or dictatorial may emanate from this role or concept of elevated minister. It may be more pronounced in men than women pastors for two reasons: men have a longer history at this business and they have occasionally suffered from an assumed emasculation — an unspoken and suspicious idea that the role of minister is not masculine.

Humor

There remain a few people who feel humor is out of place in the pulpit. A few Sundays after arriving at a new church one of the women visited with me after church and said she did not appreciate my humor in the pulpit. I replied I had heard the previous pastor had a great sense of humor. She said, "But not in the pulpit."

Perhaps my humor is a little warped; my wife tells me so. On two occasions when having my eyes examined I could see the examiner out in front readying the lens contraption that I was peering through. I said in a peek-a-boo sing-song fashion, "I seeee you." Both times I was met with a strange look. My wife said, "I warned you." Knowing that will help you with this book. If you encounter an occasional strange comment you don't understand, chalk it up to a pitiful attempt at humor. I have included a few jokes that I hope fit the subject. A humorous illustration should be illustrious. Phrases or expressions can be comic, droll, facetious, absurd, clever, or sarcastic. Droll, facetious, and sarcastic run the greatest risk of being misunderstood.

Humor is attention getting, however, by the same token it can be distracting. It always bothered me when the congregation continued to laugh a little too long after my joke. I was ready to get on with the serious business and they weren't listening. Many preachers enjoy a funny story or a humorous beginning that may be totally unrelated to the subject, but functions as an icebreaker or establishes rapport, which is valuable in itself. A congregation seems to enjoy a preacher directing humor at him or herself. I always had the greatest response when I was the butt of my own humor. Of course, it cannot be self-denigrating and must be in good taste.

Jokes can make a controversial subject seem more palatable or ease the tension, though those subjects are not generally conducive to humor, which may be inappropriate. Use caution.

Odds And Ends

Again, as in the first book's introduction, I apologize for the overuse of the Gospel of Matthew. I always had good intentions of reading the rest of the Bible someday. Of course, our preaching should center on the life and teachings of Jesus, but not to the exclusion of the other biblical books.

One of my intentions was to be as inclusive as possible and cover all subjects or topics on which we should preach. If you don't find a subject in this book, it may be found in the first book. There is a subject or topic index at the end of each book, and sermons may be found under multiple listings. Likewise, there will be material covered in the introduction to the first book not found in this introduction.

Remember, the sermon notes are abbreviated due to condensing for space. Also, at points I share sermon ideas for preaching or teaching, while at other times I simply give directions for the speaker for preparation. (Example: "Start by making maps to hand out or as bulletin inserts" used in sermon W-1, "Finding Your Way From Nazareth To Jerusalem.") I haven't tried to clutter the material with some method of indication to note the difference, as it is probably obvious in each case. Finally, some material is presented in the first person singular as if I am preaching it.

Since you were thoughtful enough to buy this second volume, I included two extra bonus sermons at the end.

THE LOCKHORNS

"THE PREACHER WANTS TO KNOW WHAT YOU'VE BEEN UP TO, LEROY... HE'S HAVING A HARD TIME COMING UP WITH A SERMON."

By permission of William Hoest Enterprises, Inc. and King Features Syndicate.

P.

P-1. What's The Point Of Living?

Purpose Statement: *Why are we here and what should be our goals or purpose for life?*

I'm sure you have occasionally encountered someone, often elderly, who will say, "I am still living, so God must have a reason for me still being here, but I haven't figured out what that reason is yet." This concern goes to the heart of what life is all about (note a related sermon idea X-9, "Why In The World Is There A World?"). Ecclesiastes 5:8 to 6:12, concerning goal setting and purpose for life, is a much ignored Bible passage that should be dealt with at some point. The sentiments are very pessimistic, dismal, and morbid. How do we interpret or explain this reading? We could say the author is simply posing a philosophical question and answering it by suggesting the usual pursuits of the common folk — wealth, comfort, conquests, and such — are not sufficient. But our point is to find a positive purpose for our life in the light of these melancholy expressions encountered occasionally in others, as well as in ourselves.

The question, "Why are we here?" as mentioned above is approached from a particular, specific, task-oriented position such as: "Am I supposed to find a cure for cancer, write a book, convert a certain person to Christ, or found an institution?" Perhaps our concern should be a larger and more general question, "What is the over-arching purpose for life?" Some answers could be:
    a. To enjoy life. Does this sound hedonistic? I'm sorry, but this may very well be one of God's reasons for giving us life. Genesis 1:24-31 tells of God's love in giving us existence and consciousness. We are meant to experience joy, satisfaction, and pleasure in life. That is why the world has so much beauty (flowers, sunsets, great music, and the like) and so much potential love. That is why there are beautiful relationships as we learn to share life with others.

b. To mature. We can avoid the pessimism of Ecclesiastes as we grow beyond the superficial pleasures of life and find the more mature satisfactions. One of our ultimate goals is to know God and God's will. We can grow to appreciate the lasting satisfactions that result from sacrifice and work, in contrast to the more shallow, immediate, and selfish gratifications that are more glitter and sparkle, and less substance.
c. To help others. There is greater joy in serving and loving others than in entertaining selfish ambitions. The great commandment (Luke 10:27) to love God with all we have, and our neighbor as we love our self, is at the heart of the purpose for life. This is what brings joy and pleasure. We must not be afraid to affirm that a significant purpose of our life is our enjoyment and appreciation of this world, as well as sharing that experience with others as we build beautiful relationships.

P-2. Did Jesus Really Yell At A Tree?

Purpose Statement: *As Christians are we the worker bees or the drones?*

Certain scripture passages are inexplicable, or almost so. Such a passage is Matthew 21:18-22 where we find a hungry Jesus passing by a fig tree, and because it has no figs to eat, he kills the tree. Matthew seems to use this story as an opportunity to have Jesus say that we are capable of greater things than we imagine. But, the question on all our minds is, "Would Jesus really get angry at a tree or kill a tree to teach a lesson?" It does seem out of character. Mark 11:12-14, 20-25 relates the same incident with these added details: it is not the season for the tree to bear fruit, and the tree does not immediately die, but is dead the next day when they again pass by. This story is another example of the many parallel stories of events in the ministry of Jesus that were remembered in different ways. It certainly is out of character for Jesus to kill a healthy fig tree when it isn't even fig season, in a land where there are many hungry people. We must search for other explanations. If we move to the third gospel we may find a more likely way it could have happened. Luke 13:6-9 seems to give a more reasonable account: Jesus does not kill a tree but tells a parable with excellent moral values.

    a. God wants our lives to be purposeful. The tree's owner says it hasn't produced figs for three years now; if it isn't going to bear, cut it down. Intrinsically, each of us is worth more than we can imagine. Our value as human beings is priceless; even though, at times, we are capable of acting like parasites. We shouldn't simply occupy space and use resources indiscriminately without remuneration. Occasionally, we hear some famous athlete or other celebrity say, "I need to give back to my home community for the support I received when I was just starting out." The United States is often criticized for using far more than its share of the world's natural resources. Do we give back fairly? As individual Christians we must ask ourselves if we are soaking up the abundant life or if we contribute our fair share for others. Do we give volunteer service, donate blood, help out neighbors, or take advantage of other countless opportunities to make our communities safe and pleasant? It is more than having an occupation and earning a living. Christian service goes far beyond the eight-hour-a-day job.

    b. God will give us second chances. The gardener seems like a caring and sensible individual (of course he or she does, in this story the gardener represents God) and recommends waiting one more year to see if the tree will come around. God is so generous with us because God loves us more than we can understand. God forgives us, and grants us continual opportunities to change and grow. The obvious danger is that we may be tempted to think we are able to take advantage of God's patience by irresponsible behavior. "God will always forgive us." We are unable to see the damage it does to our spirits if in another year we still haven't produced figs. We will have lost opportunities and destroyed some of our potential to serve. Our resources are not inexhaustible. We may choose to waste time and talent and watch our lives wither clear down to the roots.

P-3. Plays Well With Others: B+

Purpose Statement: *If nothing else, the Christian should be congenial, amicable, and much better at getting on well with others than most nonChristians.*

One of the most beautiful passages in scripture has to be Romans 12. If you don't agree, then go back to sleep. (Did I say that? My grade just dropped to B-.) As a description of personal conduct and interpersonal relationships, it would be difficult to find a finer list of do's and don'ts. Every Christian should start each day with a prayerful consideration of this chapter. In the midst of such lofty ideas concerning offering ourselves as living sacrifices and feeding our enemies, we find this simple clear admonition: do all you can to get along with everyone (v. 18). Christians should receive at least a B+, if not an A, on that one. Our conduct must be exemplary and impeccable. Of the many virtues listed in this chapter we could select three or four on which to elaborate. We must be ...
    a. Congenial. Of all persons, the Christian should be the easiest to get along with in ordinary circumstances. It seems to be a far too common complaint that workplace environments are beset with strained relationships. We hear of so many incidents where disharmony exists due to people who are impossible to work with or for. People who are irritable or irritating, complaining, blaming, jealous, backbiting, and the like, make our jobs so unpleasant. Christians should be the leaven, the salt (not as in irritating the wounds), the light, and the person who understands, listens, cares, and helps. Our presence in the work place or anywhere else should be a calming, consoling, reassuring element.

b. Conscientious. Saying a Christian is easy-going and pleasant does not mean we are doormats or unprincipled. It is possible to be loving and kind and at the same time uncompromising in our standards. We must have integrity and always maintain unimpeachable ethical behavior. An illustration comes to mind of a group of high school boys who would, with the illegal help of an adult, get beer after ball games. In the group there was one boy who, after the game and before the drinking began, always insisted he be dropped off at home. Yet this boy's friendship with the group was never diminished; he could maintain his integrity and his friendship at the same time. Romans 12:2 says we must not conform to the standards of this world.

c. Candid. If we care to examine the above example more closely, that boy could be accused of not being conscientious enough. Perhaps he should have been more candid or honest in the situation and done what was necessary to stop the illegal and potentially dangerous activity by reporting it. We don't give him anything better than a C+. He was young and lacked the more mature judgment you and I would exercise. Verses 7 and 8 speak of serving, teaching, and encouraging. This would include being honest with our friends. It means telling them (humbly of course — v. 16) what they need to hear but don't want to hear. One of the most difficult things we have to do — perhaps the "living sacrifice" part — is to not let any immorality or harmful conduct go unchallenged. It may cost us friendships, even though we do it congenially with kindness and love.

d. Charitable. Further into this chapter from Romans, we are instructed in the ultimate in Christian love. Out of the many acts of love, the supreme example is to love an enemy (vv. 17-21) even when it means we lay down our life for another. For this we earn an A+.

P-4. Let Me Tell You What You Believe

Purpose Statement: *So many Christians are ignorant concerning the beliefs and doctrines of their faith. A little education seems appropriate not only to enlighten but also to encourage further study.*

Some Christians have a doctrine carefully worked out, memorized, and are out there ready to proselytize. Often that doctrine or "faith" may not be very deep and that person can easily become confused when they are confronted with a few challenging questions that depart from familiar territory. However, many of us don't know enough about our faith to begin to ask those profound questions, let alone answer difficult questions. We may be in serious need of a more mature grasp of the Christian faith and biblical theology. The writer of Hebrews (5:11—6:3) tells us we are like babes who still must drink milk, whereas we should have been mature enough for solid food by now. Hebrews seems to have been written for Christians who were just "getting by" in the church. They were lukewarm in the faith, and perhaps in danger of abandoning it altogether. A mature faith must begin with our knowing what it is all about. Let me tell you what you believe.

a. Common Christian beliefs that unite us. (The pastor should give a skeleton outline of the central teachings of the Christian faith.) We believe in one God, in Jesus the revelation of God, in prayer, in eternal life, in love and forgiveness, and in the Bible as one source (along with prayer, the spirit of God in our lives, and the witness of other Christians) of our knowledge of God and God's will for us.

b. Beliefs unique to our particular church. (The pastor needs to expand on what differentiates a Presbyterian, Lutheran, Baptist, Methodist, and other denominations from other Christians.) As a particular denomination, we hold beliefs about what baptism and communion mean and how they are administered. Beliefs concerning orders in the church — deacons, bishops, and so forth — may be unique to our denomination. What membership means and who are members, how we are saved, what constitutes worship, healing, speaking in tongues, who has authority and what kind, needs clarifying, as we also stress tolerance and respect for other traditions as important.

c. How we arrive at those beliefs. Generally, there are two approaches by which we arrive at our personal beliefs, although the journey is usually a blend of the two. We can be taught (or told) by the powers that be, the hierarchy of the church, what we are supposed to believe, or we can search the scriptures, pray, study, and join classes as we "work out our own faith." Something "handed" to us is usually never as meaningful as that which we have arrived at through personal struggle. The former method allows the church to "keep control" of theology and maintain original and orthodox positions. The latter permits a certain amount of danger that we may stray into strange or even bizarre paths. Of course, the church should provide direction and focus to our personal searches.

P-5. No Yellow Flags!

Purpose Statement: *Christians should be concerned about avoiding making mistakes.*

Quite often, while watching a football game, we may become frustrated when a player on "our" team makes a mistake and the official throws a yellow flag on the ground. It seems to happen to "our" team, and never to the other team when they have a drive going. They are moving the ball down the field and then a penalty sets them back and stalls out the momentum. Doesn't it always seem the penalty is foolish and avoidable? A lineman jumps offside before the ball is snapped or a player blocks from behind. As spectators, we consider these ridiculous mistakes should never happen except to players on the other team who are not smart enough to avoid them. It should be so easy: just don't jump offside. The same thing happens to all of us, probably daily, as we make foolish mistakes and God (thinking, "How stupid can that human be?"), wants to throw a yellow flag.

    a. Christian concern. The teachings of Jesus are filled with concern for others to the extent we must consider it one of the major themes. We are to be Good Samaritans, feed the poor, go the second mile, be peacemakers, heal others, and love our neighbor as our self. Logically, it follows we should avoid making mistakes that inconvenience or hurt others. This must become one of our major concerns and is the reason for this sermon. As our world gets more crowded and complicated, there are more and more mistakes being made every day. We live in an age of information and communication, and yet errors seem to occur now more than ever. Jesus' parable of the ten attendants at the wedding (Matthew 25:1-11) is apropos of our daily experiences. Five of them were careless and spoiled the wedding. Christians must avoid mistakes.

    b. Serious concern. Most of our errors are minor and many are harmless, which makes them insidious in their accumulative affect on social harmony. For example, when we order something by mail, often we will not get what we ordered. While many mistakes may only inconvenience someone (which a Christian does not want to do at any time), they may also be of life and death proportions. How often have we heard of an accident where a person ran through a red light and killed someone in another car? One story told of a compounding error where the emergency vehicle was sent to the wrong location by the dispatcher who gave the address in the 1600 block and the accident was in the 600 block. The injured person might have lived had the ambulance arrived on time. Being accident prone or careless may become habitual simply because we have not conditioned or disciplined ourselves. Jesus told a parable (Matthew 25:14-23) about being faithful in small matters and being rewarded with greater responsibilities. Can we turn this coin over and make it applicable to our

mistakes? If we are careless in little things like jumping offside, could we be conditioning ourselves for more serious penalty flags such as unnecessary roughness?
c. Remedial concern. As a Christian, I must care enough to do my best. My concern for others should motivate me to remedial action in exercising care and thoughtfulness at all times since some occasions are of a life and death nature. A part of our spiritual exercise each day should include preparation in carefulness. We can practice avoiding accidents and mistakes just as industry and businesses hope to prevent or curtail injuries on the job by posting signs in the workplace stating: "We are in our 38th accident-free day." God wants me to tell you that I will be very cautious because I love you. A person who lived at the top of a mountain accessible only by a tortuous winding road with steep drop-offs was interviewing chauffeurs. The first applicant drove very fast to make an impression of how skilled he was. The second applicant drove very close to the edge of the drop-offs to show how brave a driver she was. The third applicant drove very slowly and as far from the edge as possible, and was the one hired.

P-6. God Always Wins At Hide And Seek

Purpose Statement: *We can't get away from God.*

A Texas man, bragging to an acquaintance about how big his ranch was, tried to illustrate by saying, "I can get in my pickup and drive for three hours and still not get to the other side of my property." She replied, "I have a pickup like that." God's neighborhood is even bigger and our pickups are even more inadequate. We cannot move away. Psalm 139 is a favorite of many. God knows all our thoughts (v. 2). God is all around us (v. 5). Where could we possibly go to escape from God (v. 7)? We can't hide in the dark (v. 11). We must submit to God (vv. 23-24). The early Hebrews believed God was local, and then, for a while, God was confined to a mountaintop. God finally moved into a box and then a temple. It took a Jeremiah and an Ezekiel to tell us we can worship God everywhere because God is everywhere, even in Babylonian captivity.

    a. Our hiding. Whether extrovert or introvert we all like to have quiet private time and would dislike very much to have intrusions in those moments. Sometimes we want to get away from it all and be alone. There may be other specific reasons for our avoiding God.

        1. Why? It might be very much like not wanting to face a spouse, a friend, or a boss when we have screwed up some responsibility, didn't even get started on a task, or know that we are going to be asked to do something we dread. Even knowing the confrontation is inevitable sooner or later, we still try to avoid the face-to-face show down.

        2. How? Since Psalm 139 reveals God's ubiquitous nature, the almost universal hiding place of popular choice is simply to pretend God isn't there. If we simply don't think about God we believe we won't have to deal with what God wants us to do and not do.

    b. God's seeking. The life and ministry of Jesus was totally geared to reconciling us to our creator God.

        1. Compelling. We think we don't need God in our lives until an emergency occurs. We assume we get along better without God's interference because we think we have been doing so well. Even when we know parenting is frustrating us, the work place is stressing, and too many things go wrong, we won't admit our need for God. Yet our need for God is shadowing us incessantly. God desires a relationship (creator with creature, as parent with child), in order that we may become fulfilled and become more aware of God's love and forgiveness. The cross compels us to acknowledge God's constant overture to us.

        2. But not obtrusive. In God's great wisdom and perfect universe, there is that delicate balance between God's love wooing us and God's respect for our privacy. In

the final analysis, as Psalm 139 makes so clear, though God is all around us and inescapable, it remains for us to invite God (vv. 23-24) into our lives. God loves us so much while respecting our freedom and privacy, that strangely enough, even to our own possible destruction, we remain totally free to our dangerous devices. The redeeming feature is that ultimately we have eternal life, as the prodigal son parable makes amply clear.

P-7. Should Acolytes Wear Sneakers?

Purpose Statement: *How formal or informal should we allow our worship services to become?*

It is difficult to believe some of the things that have been seen or heard in our traditional Sunday morning worship services. Some of the innovative activities or foolish incidents, depending on your perspective, done in the name of being modern or getting people's attention certainly must go beyond good taste or appropriate worship. Where do we draw the line? We all remember Jesus going into the temple at Jerusalem (John 2:13-17) and getting angry over moneychangers and the presence of cattle as improper for meaningful worship. The incident is found in all four gospels, and records Jesus saying the house of worship had become a den of thieves and a marketplace. John 2:17 expresses the sentiments that our devotion for God's house should burn within us like a fire. Isaiah 6 likens worship in the temple unto an awesome and very holy experience. Moses (Exodus 3:5) is instructed to remove his shoes, for being in God's presence is like standing on holy ground. Exodus 28:1-14 describes how the priests are to dress for temple worship with gold and precious gem stones because worship of God is to be stately, awe-inspiring, and regal. Exodus 40 elaborates on the anointing and consecration of worship and worship things. Verses 34 and 35 tell us that because of God's presence in the tent of worship, Moses could not even enter. As a contrast, in many churches, on Sunday morning we see the candlelighters wearing lovely formal robes with sneaker accessories peeking out from the bottom of the robe. You may have been at one of those weddings where male attendants were decked out in formal tuxedos complete with matching work boots or sneakers. The major question we all should ask ourselves is, "What is appropriate and what isn't?" Clearly there have been some performances in our worship services that have gone over the edge. What is, and what isn't, appropriate?

    a. Purpose of worship. Perhaps some questions to begin with would be: What is God like and what are we doing when we worship? Why are you here this morning and what do you expect to happen? The answers to these kinds of questions would go a long way toward dictating what constitutes a meaningful worship environment.

    b. Dignity and respect. We stand at attention, remove our caps, and place our hands over our hearts for the flag (perhaps bordering on the idolatrous), but how do we give respect to God and dignity to our worship? Our modern choruses place almost exclusive emphasis on praising God, and how awesome God is, while our posture and demeanor may belie this attitude. And yet, God is a God of joy and excitement. Our worship should include humor, joyfulness, celebration, and creativity. Finding that appropriate balance is the secret.

    c. Formality. Back to the sneakers. How formal should we dress to express the respect we desire and the devotion we feel? Are T-shirts, short shorts, jeans (with or without holes), and the like, acceptable or too tacky? The concern that quickly comes to mind is that some persons do not have "nice" clothes and we certainly want them to feel comfortable coming to church with whatever they have. We have quite a dilemma: clothes affect us psychologically — our attitudes and how we behave — and yet there are persons who cannot afford to dress with anything approaching formality and we want them to feel welcome.

d. Propriety. One of the concerns at the last church I served was over proper conduct upon entering the sanctuary. Some members wanted silence to prepare prayerfully for worship. Others wanted it to be a time of greeting and friendliness. Both seemed to be appropriate postures, and yet the issue seemed small potatoes compared with the distractions we often encounter today. We go back to the fundamentals and ask what kind of activity, dress, and behavior will be most conducive for us to worship meaningfully.

P-8. Mom, Where Did We Come From?

Purpose Statement: *Occasionally a sermon on who we are, historically, would be appropriate.*

A small girl asked her mother where she came from. Her mother went into great detail explaining conception and birth and when she finished, her daughter said, "Mom, I only wanted to know where we lived before we moved to this house." The church has a rich, though checkered, history. Because many Christians have too loose a connection with their church, it behooves us not only to strengthen our relationship with God, Jesus, and our church, but also to give us some historic identity. Hebrews 12:1-2 speaks about our rich heritage that demands our own courageous and exciting commitment. Yet, many people know so little about the church they attend, hard as that is to believe. Though they attend a Presbyterian, Baptist, Methodist, Lutheran, or other church steeped in historic tradition, they know next to nothing about that rich history. Unfortunately, some local churches don't have those rich connections to celebrate, but they still have a limited history with which to identify.
 a. Present the particular denomination's history, including its great leaders, and institutions (such as schools and hospitals).
 b. Share the doctrines and beliefs that gave birth to the denomination, which are distinctive from other churches, as well as those we all share in common.

c. Tie in the relationship to the church over the centuries with its origins in Jesus, either as a part of this sermon or a second one in a series.

P-9. One Bible — So Many Churches!

Purpose Statement: *Why are there so many different denominations?*

There are so many different churches believing so many different things and some of them are quite eccentric. It started early on in Paul's day with the churches going different directions. In 1 Corinthians 1:10-17 Paul criticizes the divisions in the early church and suggests that we should be united in our faith. Again, in Ephesians 4:1-6, he encourages unity saying that there is only one body, one Spirit, one hope, one faith, one God. And again, in Galatians 1:6-9, Paul claims there is only one gospel to proclaim, but some are preaching "another gospel." I believe the great variety of churches and beliefs represent a scandal for Christianity. We find ourselves unable to cooperate or present a united witness to the world. We are so estranged over our beliefs that we cannot have a fellowship together. Clergy have to have different social groups, unable even to eat together. The July 20, 2002, news carried a story concerning a denomination that suspended one of its clergy for participating in an interfaith service for families of those killed in the attacks on the World Trade Center. We should be actively engaged in learning about one another and what we can do to grow closer in our faith. Yet, little or nothing is being done. We must start with the reasons we are so divided. Among others they would include:

    a. Biblical interpretation. The problem begins here. Most of our differences stem from how we perceive the Bible. Some understand the Bible to be infallible, perfect, dictated by God and needing to be protected from any change or challenges. This generally means that scripture should be taken literally. Others believe scripture was written by fallible human beings, contains some contradictions and errors,

and should be interpreted in different ways: myth, history, figuratively, literally, and some of it as uncertain.
  b. Self perception. Those who see scripture as perfect will usually view themselves as having the only true understanding or interpretation. They tend to see their church as the only true church, while all others are seriously mistaken in their faith. On the other hand, those who find the Bible fallible will also believe they have a theology containing both some truth and some mistaken notions. This necessitates a constant effort to gain greater understanding. They are more likely to be tolerant towards others with different doctrines, recognizing them as sisters and brothers in Christ. They will say no one has the corner on the truth.
  c. Major ministry. The first group described — those who see the Bible as perfect and think they are the exclusive keepers of the truth — generally see their task as saving the world which translates into winning souls over to "their way." Nothing is as important as winning people for Christ. The second group — those who know they do not have all the truth — have a propensity to see their ministry in terms of serving people and trying to create a better world for all of us to live in. Neither group would be pleased with these descriptions of themselves however much such descriptions may be general in nature.

We are not so easily divided into categories as the above suggests and we all have our inconsistencies, however we usually gravitate towards two general stances regarding our faith and Bible interpretation. As impossible as it seems, dialogue among Christians of different views is necessary. As long as it doesn't happen, the splintered nature of our church will continue to suffer irreparable damage in its witness and ministry.

P-10. Guns Яn't Us

Purpose Statement: *We must explore whether guns are worth the cost of life and limb.*

(Some readers will go "ballistic" over this message. But then, you still have 111 other palatable sermon ideas left that will make you one of the most popular preachers in town, unless one of your colleagues down the street also buys this book. However, that preacher may choose to use this sermon idea, and then you'll be back on top once more.) The scripture that seems appropriate is Matthew 26:52b, where Jesus says that if we use guns we will die by guns. He actually said swords, but I'm sure he meant guns. Since I am a Christian pacifist, you would expect my position to be one of anti-violence at every turn. However, this message is not concerned with war, but doing what will create the most responsible and safe circumstance for you, your family, and friends. That is one of the major concerns of the Christian: to be considerate of others and solicitous for their safety and well-being. Consequently the reason for this sermon is to offer another opportunity to do something to show love for others by our concern for their protection.

    a. Why have guns? There are at least three reasons:
        1. Hunting. There may be two reasons why we hunt: food and sport. Obviously we no longer need to hunt to eat. Regarding "sport," we all need to take a more serious look at what we are doing when we hunt. Do we enjoy killing life just for "sport"? An otherwise very good and sensitive person (we always hear: "he or she is a very good family person and a responsible citizen") will have certain weaknesses that need to be examined and rectified. Why does a person find satisfaction or enjoyment out of taking life? It would seem we could find greater satisfaction from hunting with a camera including just as much excitement and challenge. Photographs would make pleasant mementos instead

of spoils afterward. Enhance your already sensitive side with becoming one with life and not destructive of life.
   2. Protection. This almost seems a legitimate reason. Protection from what? Two enemies come to mind: intruders or criminals, and the government. Yes, I said government. There are gun owners who insist it is important to maintain an arsenal just in case the government comes to get you. I am still trying to tie this one in with patriotism and pride in our democracy. But don't we need to have a gun to keep robbers out of our homes and muggers from assaulting us on the streets? One statistic gleaned from the United Methodist magazine, *The Interpreter*, April 1988, (p. 32) tells us a study of FBI records revealed that our personal handgun is 118 times more likely to be used in a murder, suicide, or fatal accident than it will be used to kill a criminal! If odds mean anything to us, we are in greater danger of injuring or killing ourselves, a family member, or a friend, than in protecting our selves from criminals. Do you really keep a loaded gun accessible in your home?
   3. Hobby. Gun collecting may be interesting, but there are certain things that simply cost too much to maintain. Do we want to pay such a high price in human life by keeping such destructive elements around us when they are superfluous and useless (similar to smoking, gambling, owning a vicious dog, or using alcohol)?
   4. Adolescent defiance. "I have my rights!" (Okay, so don't use this one.)
b. Why not to have guns? If the above discussion hasn't moved you, then consider what Jesus may have meant when he said, "If you use the sword, you will die by the sword." (Use statistics here that you gather from current research.)
   1. The United States has more personal and private gun ownership than most any other country in the world, which should make us one the safest countries, yet we

have far more personal violence with guns than any other country in the world. Our gun homicide rate (deaths per 100,000 people) is far higher than any other country in the world, and this does not include accidents with guns!
2. During the Vietnam war there were more than twice as many United States citizens killed with guns in our own country than in combat in Vietnam.
3. Guns are the fifth leading cause of death of our children in this country.
4. 92 percent of burglaries occur in unoccupied homes.
5. Homes are broken into to get guns! Roughly 80 percent of guns used by criminals are stolen from gun owners. It is the gun owners who are arming the criminals.
6. Studies show a woman carrying a gun in her purse for protection is more likely to have it used against her than to use it herself.

As Christians who love people and want a safer society, we should consider the abolition of guns, or at the least, greater gun control laws. We would not be entirely honest if we did not deal with Luke 22:35-38 where Jesus appears to instruct his followers to buy swords. This difficult passage (v. 37) is cryptic and perhaps full of sarcasms and exasperation. When two disciples say they have two swords, Jesus replies, "That is enough!" (note the exclamation point in the text) which also could be interpreted as, "Enough of this!" or "Enough, enough!" Is Jesus saying, "Stop being ridiculous; don't you understand what I am saying? I don't mean literally buy swords. What would you do with them? Don't you understand my ministry by now?" Remember the context of our text (Matthew 26:52).

Q.

Q-1. Ate With Any Wicked People Lately?

Purpose Statement: *As Christians are we allowed to associate with "bad" people?*

   I believe this question is more relevant than we imagine. Our world is all mixed up with different kinds of people, some of whom do some very bad things. Contact with persons of "questionable" character, persons who are very dishonest, or even downright criminal is unavoidable. We have neighbors and coworkers who can be immoral or criminal and we must respond in some fashion. Perhaps this is more of a vital concern for youth. We want our children to "stay away" from the bad kids. They might get into trouble or be influenced by peer behavior. Even though there may not be any actual behavior problems and our children could be quite innocent, it is still possible to attain a reputation by casual or assumed association. Many times I have heard parents protest that their children are the good ones who simply "got in with the wrong crowd." It is intriguing to consider the possibility that in some cases the parents of each youth in "the crowd" feels the same way. Who, then, would be the "bad crowd"? The advice is to stay away from bad people, and yet we are told by Jesus himself that he was accused of associating with evil people as Matthew 11:19 records. It sounded like he even partied with them. Jesus certainly sat down and ate socially with the wicked (Luke 15:2). We have no good reason to question the accuracy of the charge; it was Jesus' way and he even told parables affirming this. If Jesus did it, shouldn't we follow his example?
   a. Who are these bad people? The first mistake to be avoided is judging and assuming more than we should. We are told not to judge others. In some instances we have no real evidence of the character of a person and may be reacting on gossip or false reputation. At times we are ignorant of extenuating circumstances that if known would change our

evaluation of the entire situation. We must also remember that one bad deed, or an area of weakness in a person, does not make that individual a bad person. Which brings us to the dangerous assumptions that we are "good" people. Remember, Jesus asked us to remove the log from our own eye first before dealing with the faults of others. There is one safe assumption to make, we are all a mix of good and bad in varying degrees. Recognizing our own sinfulness is paramount to setting the course of our own crusade to save others.

b. Aren't we supposed to love them? There are so many ways to misunderstand the word "love." One may think loving our enemies or other people in general means to be personally connected with them. We don't have to party with, or become best friends with, persons in order to love them. In this case, love means being kind, helping when we can, and working for the best interest of others. Sometimes we may be called to take some risks, but generally we can *love* others from a safe distance if situations call for it. We can see that individuals, even dangerous individuals, can receive help without any contact at all. In other cases, it is appropriate to make a witness through contact and direct action.

c. Where do we draw the lines? This is a question not easily answered; nevertheless one necessarily unavoidable at times. How dangerous would association with a specific individual be? How bad is that person? What does Christian love direct us to do? What can we safely do? Because this often requires careful judgment, you and I would be very wise to consult with other Christians. We must do what is loving for others and yet safe for all concerned.

d. Are we strong enough? Each of us has our strengths and weaknesses. Could our associations with an alcoholic, an overeater, or an individual with a sex problem tempt us? Where is safe ground for us? Are we far enough along in our faith journey to make the kind of contacts needed in particular situations and not stumble if we are to be loving witnesses?

Q-2. When Your Friends Are Naughty

Purpose Statement: *How do we act when our friends do wrong things?*

The differentiation between this message and the previous one is that here we are concerned with friends and even family members, not the "bad crowd." Examples to illustrate the concern would include: How do you make the proper response when a friend tells a racist joke, engages in inappropriate behavior, suggests questionable activities, gossips, or reveals something illegal they have done? There are occasions when differences will separate family or friends as in when Jesus said, "he came to bring a sword" (see sermon O-7, "How Good Was Jesus With A Sword?"). But this separation comes when we are pushed away, not because we pull away. We love and stick by our friends. But, there are some uncomfortable scriptures that must be considered. In Matthew 18:15-17, Jesus seems to suggest severe treatment toward "sinners." Certainly this passage needs to be placed in context with his teachings concerning not judging, loving enemies, turning the other cheek, the prodigal son, and many others where Jesus apparently tells us to support our friends. Perhaps his harsh injunctions were intended to guard against condoning the sin (see point "b" below). In 1 Corinthians 5:9-13, Paul extends the stand-off treatment a little farther when he tells us not to associate with brothers and sisters who continue to sin. Again, this may be an effort to avoid the appearance of condoning the sin. Paul doesn't even give the instruction to help them before abandoning them as Jesus suggests. Of course, like Jesus' teaching in the Matthew passage cited above, Paul's strong word of condemnation must be set in the midst of his many teachings concerning helping and loving sinners. I think Jesus and Paul would concur with the following three suggestions.

    a. Thou shalt not compromise. This means compromise in the sense of giving up one's own principles to be accepted by the group or the "sinner." Don't be led astray or be tempted to violate your own standards of moral conduct. We don't emulate the conduct of whomever we happen to be with. I don't believe that "when in Rome do as the Romans do" is biblical. Jesus said that his disciples are not of the world (John 17:16). The principles that regulate our conduct are not the world's standards, but God's way.

b. Thou shalt not condone. Even though we may not participate with family or friends in inappropriate behavior, our posture of silence can give the impression of accepting or approving instead of condemning. Consider one of the illustrations mentioned above: a friend telling a racist joke. We don't tell or repeat such jokes, but when we laugh or simply fail to make some kind of protest, we have given permission for such behavior. We must find tactful and loving, but unequivocal, ways to register our disapproval of improper activities — not an easy task. The father in the prodigal son story did not reprimand his sinful son and yet there was an unspoken understanding built into that situation that the son had done wrong and foolish things. It was acknowledged by the son's comments. There was no question that his father condoned his profligate behavior by celebrating his homecoming. When Jesus forgave the woman caught in adultery (John 8:1-11) he was not approving or excusing it. He said, "Go, and sin no more."

c. Thou shalt not condescend. It is easy and even fun to look down on sinners from a superior position of saintliness, don't you think? We should continually remind ourselves that Jesus said to take the beam out of our own eye before we help find the speck in someone else's eye. In the adulterous woman story, Jesus said that the person without sin could cast the first stone. No one stepped forward and I assume you and I wouldn't have been able to either. (It is rumored that one woman did stoop to pick up a stone, and Jesus had to admonish, "Now, Mom!") Let us always be careful that our attitude isn't one of "holier than thou." Self-righteous demeanor is neither helpful nor appreciated. We don't give up our friends. We don't condone or emulate their bad conduct. Instead, we join hands together as sinners in mutual support and love.

Q-3. Love Your Neighbor — Very Carefully!

Purpose Statement: *It is important to remind our church family to not allow ourselves to be placed in jeopardy by doing good deeds.*

The Good Samaritan story (Luke 10:25-37) is one of the most famous and favorite that Jesus told. This, despite the fact that it asks a tremendous sacrifice of each one of us. A "teacher of the Law" inquires about the "love your neighbor as yourself" part of the Great Commission (this is another version of the Golden Rule). When the teacher asks Jesus who is his neighbor, Jesus answers with the Good Samaritan parable. If the principle lesson of the story is that we should help others, the ancillary idea is that love and service knows no class, religious, ethnic, or such restrictions. Everyone is a sister or brother and a neighbor to us. (The story mentions it was "religious leaders" who passed by without helping the victim. Pastors love to say, "they saw the man was *already* robbed and so went on their way.) There is a serious and valuable addendum to this story each pastor must share. We must be very careful that being a Good Samaritan doesn't put us in danger.

    a. It's mandatory. We cannot argue with the idea that it is God's will that we love each other, and this means helping others out of difficulties wherever we can. Once a state trooper saw me pulled over at the side of the road with a flat tire. He made a U-turn, came back, and would not let me change my tire. He insisted on doing it for me so I would not get my suit and tie ensemble soiled. Jesus made it clear there were no conditions to that love and service. You and I must help anyone we can, even an enemy. Matthew 5:38-48, and many other passages, leave no doubt in the matter. Such good deeds make our world a much better place to live.

    b. It's dangerous. The main point of this message is that there is danger in doing good and each pastor must see to it that the Good Samaritan story comes with a warning label. One such danger is that you, or I, could inadvertently cause more harm to a person in need. Despite our intentions to help, we might accidentally injure the individual and be the recipient of a lawsuit. We cannot let the risk of being sued prevent our good deeds. Just be extra careful. There are laws on the books (coincidentally called the "Good Samaritan Laws," I believe) where you cannot be held responsible for doing harm when you were sincerely trying to do good. Know the laws of your state. However, a more insidious danger is that you may be the victim of a trap laid to rob or injure you. Occasionally, that stranded motorist, or needy person knocking on your door, doesn't really need help, but is a criminal planning to attack you. Of course, there are times when we do risk our lives to save another person. Jumping into the lake to save someone who is drowning, or rushing into a burning building to rescue someone, are examples where we may choose to risk our lives, but it is important for us to first consider other alternatives. There may be a long pole we can use to reach out to the drowning person.

c. It's doable. We can provide help in many instances in a safe way. (Here the sermon should recite a list of examples of safety precautions we should know and use. For example: If the situation doesn't look right, don't stop. Use your cell phone or the phone at the next stop to call for help for the person stranded by the road. Don't let strangers into your home to use the phone. Make the call for them. We can't stress the importance of this message enough. Our church members are not doing the "right thing" by allowing themselves to become victims of a criminal act.) There are many alternatives and safe ways to provide service to someone in need without jeopardizing our lives. God calls on us for sacrifices on occasion, but never foolish ones. It is never intended that we become the victim of crime, when there are more careful and responsible ways of being a Good Samaritan.

Q-4. Worship Is More Than Just Staying Awake

Purpose Statement: *When is worship really worship?*

If we were honest with each other, we might admit that many services of worship we have experienced have been empty and not worthy of the label, "worship." Reasons vary. A worship service may not have been conducted in a worshipful manner (we still might find something meaningful anyway); perhaps our worship has become too routine so as to make it easy to lose sight of our purpose; we may not have come to worship prepared and expectant; or other of the many reasons. There are many sermons on the topic of worship: the elements, the style, distractions within us and around us, where we can worship, preparation, intention, expectations, and so on. In Isaiah 6:1-11, Isaiah sees God in the temple. The temple shook and was filled with smoke and strange creatures symbolizing an ecstatic moment most of us haven't experienced, yet. The question each of us can ask ourselves is, "When does worship happen for us?" We might try the following imagery even if it seems rather contrived.

    a. When we are as timid as a mouse. Isaiah says there is no hope for him; he is doomed (v. 5) as a sinful person trembling in the presence of an awesome God. Real worship begins with a confession of our sinfulness. This does not mean we fear God; it means we are humble and timid in God's awesome presence. God has blessed us beyond comprehension and we have answered with apathy, rudeness, failure, hatred, greed, carelessness, or other undesirable behaviors. In remorse, we stand trembling and tearful in God's presence. We are sorry we sinned; not just that we got caught.

    b. When we are happy as a lark. After sincere repentance, we know our sins are forgiven (v. 7). We are joyful over new life and reconciliation with God. Talk about emotional swings. It can be as polar as from depression to euphoric. We may have done things, at times, that warrant some deep sorrow. Release from this kind of burden and experiencing genuine forgiveness can be immense, in contrast.

c. When we are courageous like a lion. After that kind of healing, our next emotion would be the desire to serve God as an expression of our gratitude. "God, what can we do? Give us some brave task." Isaiah hears God calling for a messenger and responds, "Here am I, send me" (v. 8). The greater the forgiveness and love is, the greater is the gratefulness, and the more courageous is our commitment to serve. There have been those times when we felt there wasn't enough we could do to thank a friend or repay an obligation. When God's presence is felt in our hearts, we are ready to roar.

d. When we become wise as an owl. God immediately gave Isaiah understanding or knowledge (v. 9), instructions on what to say to the people. We may not receive a commission similar to that of a prophet such as Isaiah, but there will be moments in our worship experience when we feel that our lives now have definite direction and purpose. We know what the task is and how we can achieve it.

e. When we become busy as a beaver. The task is awesome for Isaiah (v. 10); there is much to do and it won't be easy. Worship should be reflected in our total life; the true response to meaningful worship finds expression in a busy Christian life. Because we have worshiped on Sunday at church (or any day, any where), we commit to a life full of service and witnessing. This does not mean the reverse is true: that the person who is overly active in the life of the church family has a great devotional life. But who are we to judge?

f. When we are stubborn like a mule. As we make our way through the zoo, it is at this point that we are prone to let down. Like the parable of the two sons, one said he would go and work in the field, but didn't. A very common pattern is clearly discernable in our resolutions and commitments: We start off with a bang and then, after a while, we begin to wind down. Isaiah asks how long his responsibility is to last, and God says, "For a long time; until the cities are ruined and uninhabited" (v. 11). It is easier, at first, to get going, but persistence through discouragement, boring routine, thankless chores, and difficulties is hard to maintain. Stubborn, stick-to-it-iveness is what is wanted for God's work. Is our wake strewn with tasks left half finished? It is time to get back to the temple.

Q-5. Little Orphan Annie Complex

Purpose Statement: *We need to deal with our fear of growing old.*

"Fear" may not be the right word, however most people do not want to grow old. If we could, many of us might choose perpetual youth and become like Little Orphan Annie, Dagwood and Blondie, or their children. These folks found the fountain of youth as Annie appeared on the scene as a youth in 1924 and remained a youth ever since. Alexander and Cookie Bumstead have been children or teenagers for fifty or sixty years. The incongruity doesn't seem to bother us; what does bother us is our growing old. We can:

a. Dread it. Psalm 71 is the prayer of an old person who recognized the need for God's help as we age. We have good reason to dread getting older for age brings additional health concerns and incapacities. It is the rare person who escapes old age problems such as arthritis, vision problems, prostate complications, cancer, or other ailments. No one in their right mind wants any of those pains or inconveniences. We become more and more limited in our activities: giving up golf and driving, hearing and seeing less, and experiencing shortness of breath and weak knees. We may encounter greater health expenses and even have to leave our homes for a nursing home stay. It behooves us to reflect on the example of the old man's prayer in Psalm 71 and seek God's help. With God's help, pain and inconveniences can be a very beneficial maturing process.

b. Accept it. There is much good to aging. Proverbs 20:29 reminds us that while youth has its advantages, so does old age. This proverb suggests that there is a respect for gray hair and old age. While we haven't yet captured the Asian's appreciation for age, there is still a regard for the maturity, grace, and wisdom that we should embrace instead of running from it. We use wrinkle creams, face-lifts, pills, and exercise to perpetuate our youth. There is nothing wrong with maintaining our youthful vigor through proper exercise, continual mental activity, and diet, but it goes beyond good sense when we try to hide and deny age. We have many euphemisms such as "golden age" and "seniors" that are not inappropriate as long as it isn't denial. We preserve our youthful appearance by covering up our gray hair, which should be a crowning glory. We even have preferred euphemisms for that. We shun the word, "dye," and prefer the word, "rinse." By any other word, we are doing the same thing; the only difference is semantics. Go with the flow and enjoy whatever benefits old age brings. Retirement gives us ample opportunities for hobbies. Be sure to prepare for limited capacities by acquiring new interests that can be done when we can no longer walk or see as well: chess, music, or volunteer phoning, for instance. Leisure time advantages — no boss, not having to get up early and rush out to work in the snow, doing what you want when you want — is wonderful. I enjoy falling back on the excuse, "I'm getting old and don't remember well," when I make mistakes.
c. Welcome it. As bad as it seems at times, it is a gift from God. It brings wisdom through experience, mental maturity and preparation for an exciting new adventure — death. Peter Pan said something like, "Dying will be an awfully big adventure." Psalm 39:1-5 expresses the thought that life gets tough and the end finally brings relief. The psalmist asks when he or she will die. Life is short at any length, and Christianity has promised us the expanded consciousness of eternity, which the psalmist couldn't appreciate due

to not having the benefit of the Christian promise. We should love life, this gift from God, and cherish it always. However, we should equally appreciate the gift of our release from the physical into the spiritual world. Paul tells us that to live is wonderful, but to die is also very special (Philippians 1:20-24). He (1 Corinthians 15) elaborates on the wonderful nature of eternal life after this earthly life. Our bodies will put on the spiritual body that is beautiful, strong, and immortal (vv. 40-43). Jesus has revealed the victory to us (v. 57).

Q-6. Would Jesus Stretch The Truth?

Purpose Statement: *Jesus used exaggeration in his teaching and for good reason.*

There are some cultural differences that we must understand when trying to appreciate some of the stories in our Bible. Even Jesus used stratagems and techniques that were popular in his day. One such cultural technique was the style of emphatic exaggeration when teaching. Jesus was a master at teaching and used a great deal of exaggeration. He spoke about selling everything and giving it to the poor (Matthew 19:21), told his followers to buy a sword (Luke 22:36), said we must lose our lives in order to save them (Luke 9:24), we could drink poison (Mark 16:18), we could move mountains (Mark 11:23), he could rebuild the temple in three days (John 2:19), and many more. His listeners did not consider what he said as lying or deceit. They could understand his use of exaggeration. Important: If we don't understand his method, we may misunderstand his message! When we think about it, his reasons for exaggeration were obvious and helpful:
    a.   Get our attention. Passages such as the stars falling from heaven and the sun dying (Matthew 24:29) or our being cast into a burning hell (Matthew 13:50) were certainly uses of imagery that would catch the attention of his listeners. Anyone versed in astronomy knows today that stars

moving even at the speed of light would never be observed to move through the heavens due to their great distances from us. But using such descriptions causes us to perk up and listen.

b. Stress importance. The lessons Jesus taught were so valuable, exaggeration was used to drive the idea home with great emphasis. Camels passing through the eye of needles (Matthew 19:24) and having logs in our eyes (Matthew 7:3) lends dramatic poignancy to the ideas being considered. It is saying, "I am trying to be as emphatic as I can to tell you how important these ideas are."

c. Help us remember. When Jesus uses such visualization as swallowing camels (Matthew 23:25), plucking out our eyes or cutting our hands off (Matthew 18:8-9), or telling us he came to bring a sword and cause dissention instead of peace (Matthew 10:34-36), his rationalization was to help us retain these important ideas. Very few of his listeners could read, or had access to, written material. It was an age when history was preserved by oral tradition. By exaggeration, his teachings became vivid and unforgettable.

Q-7. A Sunday School For Adults Only!

Purpose Statement: *Sunday school is not only for children, but also perhaps even more important for adults!*

The emphasis of this sermon would be on the importance of adult church school education in contrast to the idea that Sunday school is mainly for children, an unfortunate misconception many have. (This sermon differs from the sermon Y-5, "Everything I Needed To Know I Learned In Sunday School," which emphasizes the importance of church school education over secular education: it is more important to be moral than smart.) Fortunately, Sunday school or church school education is not an either/or situation. It is not mutually exclusive. We can, and must, have both. *But, if* we

could only have one, I would argue for the value of adult education first.
- a. It is serious business. The last church I served full time had six adult classes: college age, young adults, middle age adults, older adults, elderly adults, and business and professional women. They valued adult education and had sessions on other nights in addition to Sundays. With the problems we face — broken homes, youth delinquency, drugs, crime, reckless lifestyles, and such — there is ample need for guidance, renewal, and encouragement in our lives. Why do we neglect a wonderful resource such as church school education? Two reasons seem to jump out at us.
  1. Some church members don't really believe Sunday school can offer help for life's critical problems.
  2. That misconception grows out of the fact that the church passes up the opportunity to offer the valuable faith educational experiences that are possible.

  Some adult classes have material that is innocuous and discussion that is inane. Some of the material used in our Sunday schools leaves much to be desired; this is especially true of the adult classes. Some of our children's and youth material is excellent. Great opportunities are being squandered to have dynamic, helpful sessions about subjects that really matter. Remember how Jesus stayed back at the temple after his parents left Jerusalem when he was twelve years old (Luke 2:41-49) indicating the importance of religious education. Luke 4:16-22 indicates the value of Sabbath school as Jesus, as "usual," was in the synagogue discussing and teaching. It is a shame we so often miss excellent opportunities for church school education.
- b. It is a family affair. The reason why we might choose adult education over Sunday school for children and youth is that *in theory* if we did a good job of adult education in our churches the children and youth would receive the benefit at home. (That is if, hypothetically, we could have only one and not both.) I state this in a hypothetical fashion to emphasize the importance of reaching adults. Of course,

we are currently reaching some children and youth in our Sunday schools from homes where we will never have contact with the parents, and unfortunately much of what we accomplish on Sunday morning, in those cases, will be undone at home during the week by a dysfunctional family. For those homes where the parents are willing and concerned, it is of significant value to have the adults visit with the children and youth when they come home concerning what went on in Sunday school that morning. This reinforces the educational experience in a marvelous way.
c. It is an important example. It would be easy for children to grow up believing that church school was only for children and youth. How often do we tell children and youth to do or not to do something when we set a poor example ourselves? Use of alcohol and tobacco, no seat belts, careless driving, racist comments, cheating on taxes, and the like, are areas where we say one thing and do another. We love our children and want the best for them and yet we give them permission for destructive or inappropriate behavior by our habits. Adults taking church school seriously is a priceless influence helping our children to see religious education as a vital life-long adventure.

Q-8. Up Close And Personal

Purpose Statement: *Unfortunately, until it affects us, we usually are not willing to get involved in issues.*

What do Amos, Isaiah, Jeremiah, Hosea, Jesus, and a host of other biblical leaders have in common? Among many other things, they have in common the willingness to get involved even though they have nothing at stake, nothing personal to gain, and only a lot to lose. Some of us would ask, "What's in it for me?" before we commit ourselves. The motivation that finally caused Egypt to agree to release the Israelites is a good example of how many people respond to situations. After many plagues of boils, locusts, flies, frogs, hail, and so forth, it wasn't until the crisis became much too close to home that Egypt was moved to finally release their oppressed guests. We read in Exodus 12:29-32 how it took the death of the firstborn sons of every Egyptian family to finally move them to action. It reached every home (v. 30) and was critically personal and invasive. We are told that it was God's doing that killed these children, and conservatives will stick to that story. Liberal Christians will suggest that God had nothing to do with these deaths, but that it was some natural epidemic that was exaggerated in the telling of the details, and mistakenly attributed to God. Nevertheless, whatever happened was so close to home it stirred the people to do something. It seems this is an interesting parallel to the ways in which we so often operate. We get involved:

    a.   Only when we can identify personally with the cause. My wife and I have belonged to and supported many different organizations that deal with specific social issues. It has been our observation that many of the people who work with these organizations have decided to get involved because they have been personally connected. The following groups are ones we have not been involved with but have been familiar enough with them to observe the personal relationships. Many MADD members have had some tragic accident in their family. PFLAG workers often have a gay or lesbian in their family. Typically, persons working with cancer, alcohol, domestic abuse, and other programs have had a loved one affected, if not themselves. People naturally have more of a passion when their personal experience has caught their attention, but it also would be nice to see people volunteer for work even when they have no personal connection, except that of caring for others. How does this translate into the church? Similarly, we often don't take a sincere interest in God until it becomes personal. When a critical illness or other personal problem arises, we call on God, perhaps for the first time, seriously. When our own death is imminent, or that of a loved one, we become more interested in the prospects of salvation and eternal life.

b. Only when we are threatened. When issues arise in a community it may cause an outcry of protest. For example: school redistricting. Parents come out of the woodwork because their kids may not be going to the schools they want to attend. Or, it may be the location of group homes and businesses in neighborhoods which bring out the residents in force with the "not in my neighborhood" plea. To be very honest, most people will pay little attention to the community or national issues unless it directly affects their interests or pocketbook, and becomes personal. Often, whether it is right or wrong is not the issue, we don't want to be involved if it only touches others: "That is their problem." We tend to selfishly want what is the most convenient for us regardless of its affect on others. Again we can see the translation into the life of the church. "We've always done it this way. It's the way I am comfortable with. I don't like it that way." We need to begin considering the larger good. We mustn't live only in a world that revolves around us personally. "I don't want homeless derelicts in *my* church." But perhaps a soup kitchen is the kind of ministry this particular community needs desperately.

Q-9. There Are No Holy Wars

Purpose Statement: *There is no justification for war.*

No matter how hard we try to sanitize war, from calling missiles "peace keepers" to labeling armies "peace keeping forces," war is immoral and unnecessary. War is the simple-minded, easy way out (if you have the bigger guns) and is the immature solution. It is very much like a child saying, "You threaten me, I am going to hit you." It is a situation where we have been brainwashed over the centuries to believe in war. During a war with Babylon, Jeremiah told Jerusalem to give themselves up to the enemy (Jeremiah 28:1-6). He said to continue to resist would be fatal; if they wanted to live they should surrender. The officials wanted to put Jeremiah to death because "that kind of talk" undermined the war effort. Sound familiar? One has to do some creative interpreting of scripture to make Jesus' statement that those who use the sword will die by the sword (Matthew 26:52) mean anything other than war is wrong. Considering the entire life and ministry of Jesus, and his powerful teaching contrasting love and violence (Matthew 5:38-48), war is not a Christian option. Paul reiterates the sentiments in Romans 12:9-21. War is never justified. That war is ever necessary is the greatest misconception we may have. Consider the following points.

a. We violate even the "just war" mandates. For the first three centuries the position of the early church was one of pacifism. In the fourth and fifth centuries, as the church became politically aligned, it justified war and finally developed a "just war" set of rules. Supposedly, this set of rules has been the code ever since for conducting war. There were seven guidelines which included prohibiting attacks on noncombatants, not going to war unless a very reasonable possibility for attaining its goals exists, that it must be authorized by a legitimate authority, and it must be a last resort. In almost all conflicts today, all seven guidelines for a "just war" are seriously violated. War is immoral and unnecessary in any shape or form. However, as we choose to initiate wars, we no longer even now fight a "just" war.

b. Our "freedom" is at the expense of children killed in war. How often we hear about the brave soldiers who gave their lives for our freedom. What about the innocent women, men, and many children who are casualties of war? They were killed for our freedom. Can we feel very good about enjoying our opulent lifestyle (compared with the vast majority of the world's peoples) purchased at the cost of the lives of many children? The myth is that war "prevents so many more deaths." Consider the two atomic bombs dropped on Japan alone. We want to believe destroying those persons saved many other lives. It isn't true. Pacifism and peaceful negotiation have worked when tried!

c. War never accomplishes its purpose. World Wars I and II only exacerbated the climate of animosity and simmering revenge as they were supposed to be wars to end all wars. The later wars of the twentieth century certainly were not victories of any kind. Now we have just gone to war again urged on to attack Iraq by President Bush because Iraq "had" weapons of mass destruction. Strange that they did not use such weapons when their back was to the wall. Our recent wars have not accomplished their avowed goals, and common sense tells us future wars will fare no better. Our latest war was to stop terrorist activities, and it will only encourage future retaliation. Most people suspect that some of the reasons for war include defending our exploitive interests around the world, creating threats to keep our military and defense budget bloated, and sometimes diverting our attention from domestic problems for political advantages.

d. We ignore peaceful methods. (See sermon S-5, "Lions And Cows Dining Together: Seeing Is Believing") Because we trust in armaments instead of love, understanding, and peace, we never give the latter a chance. Essentially, we are saying God's love and the teachings of Jesus don't work. Any negotiations between nations today amount to threats. There is seldom any attempt to sincerely care about other nations and to be willing to make certain concessions as acts of good faith and trust. If we made *sincere* efforts at reconciliation, we would be surprised at the world of peace we could achieve. We dehumanize our "enemies" instead of approaching differences by mature, adult, intelligent, sharing. We can't seem to understand that much of the rest of the world sees our country as *aggressive, dangerous,* and *selfish.* Did our attack on Iraq prove them right? Can't we understand why even allies question our threatening posture? We have provoked acts of terrorist aggression against our country, here and abroad, by our attitude that we rule the world. If we were to sit down and talk with leaders of "enemy" countries and sincerely offer to provide help for their country, we would create real friends! Too many say it won't work. Consequently, that means sending soldiers overseas to die, killing countless innocent children, and antagonizing other nations to provoke more terrorist attacks on our domestic front. That has worked well! (Through serious prayer and study, every pastor must become more knowledgeable concerning the power of love and the historic successes of pacifism. My doctoral dissertation at San Francisco Theological Seminary was on pacifism and became an unbelievable eye-opener for me.)

e. There is no remorse for the enemy dead. If our intentions were honest and loving, we would show more sorrow over the massive loss of lives in war — ours, theirs, combatant, and noncombatant. We act as though people are expendable, and besides we don't know them anyway. We can always set up monuments for the dead and have a flag waving on Memorial Day. That soothes any troubled consciences anyone might have. Is there anyone anywhere who really sheds tears over the tragedy war brings to families all over the world? In its wake comes severe poverty, lost refugees, and many families who want their loved ones back alive. The cost is too great to bear and the solution Jesus offered is totally ignored!

Q-10. Pink Bunny Batteries

Purpose Statement: *How do we keep the flame burning and the enthusiasm lively?*

The slogan of the Pink Bunny who is trying to sell us batteries, is that his (I think it is a "he") batteries are long lasting. They keep you going strong. (I have heard this theme used under the title, "On Keeping On Keeping On." I liked it, but it appears to have been taken.) Recharging our batteries is what we do in the Sunday morning worship service or any worship experience, as well as in Sunday school. A central theme of the Christian faith is a constant renewing of the spirit. Two of the best passages in scripture that give us insight into that renewal are Isaiah 40:28-31 and Matthew 7:7-11. Isaiah tells us God never gets tired, but God strengthens us when we get weary. The secret is to trust in God. By doing so, we will rise up like eagles and run without getting weak. We will find that renewed energy. Jesus, in the Sermon on the Mount, assures us that if we are sincere in our seeking God and God's blessings, we will receive, we will find, and the doors will be opened. The clues all point to the same solution: sincerely desire God's presence in prayer, and trust that it will happen. The cycle is familiar.

a. Get fired up. Once upon a time there was a television program on a "rally" conducted by a famous cosmetic company reminiscent of a school pep rally. It also bordered on the religious in ardor and devotion. It was a "rah, rah" event where all the salespeople were riled up and filled with enthusiasm to get out there and sell the products that would save us all. Some were moved to emotional frenzy and I would hate to meet them five minutes later. I would have found myself buying their entire stock. You may question the motivation. Was it to make money or to give the public something they desperately needed for their well-being? Probably, it was closer to the former, but you and I as Christians have something to which nothing else can compare. Our emotional recharging experiences are few and far between sometimes. An embarrassing question might be, "Have we ever really gotten fired up?"

b. Run down. No matter how "high" (we need a new expression today) we get emotionally about our faith, it is inevitable that we will run down. The pattern is very much like a children's slide on the playground. We climb to the top and then start the descent. The Christian life can be humdrum; some tasks will be boring or unappetizing. We can start with the best of intentions (with which the road to somewhere is paved) and wind down very much like our resolutions to diet and exercise. It gets old after a while.

c. Get reenergized. I have no idea what battery company the pink bunny works for, but those batteries just keep on going. According to Isaiah and Jesus, the name of the company with the best batteries is "Trust in God." Some of the batteries available include:

1. The battery of intention. God's door will open; we only have to knock. We can't wait for anyone else to motivate us, although that happens from time to time. We must count on being intentional about it ourselves. With disciplined willpower we have to say, "Do it!" Just as hunger finally prods us into getting out of the chair, going to the refrigerator, and getting our dinner; another kind of hunger will hopefully urge us to be decisive and get going. It's time for prayer; it's time for worship; and it's time for God.

2. The battery of routine. What we need is a routine that is not routine. Routine is indispensable; we simply must not let it become too routine. Having a set time to worship or pray is important. We cannot let it get away from habit or we lose it. A nice alternative would be that we are so committed to a prayer life, and sensitive to God's presence in our lives, that we are about the business of significant worship much of the time. Without such dedication, we must rely on a daily schedule of remembering to start the day with God, and end the day with God, at a minimum. This means confession, thanks, thinking of others, listening, and the basic fundamentals. As suggested, we need a routine without a routine. It must have a built-in diversity to keep us fresh. A transfusion of new ideas and new ways is one secret to prevent a stale performance that has lost its meaning.

3. The battery of anticipation. I sincerely believe that God's glory can be found in the little things of life. When I was young, I thought I needed to vacation at Bryce Canyon, Arches National Park, or Yellowstone to really see the wonders and beauty of our world. Now that I am older, I can get just as excited about driving

through a new neighborhood. There is something wonderful in trees, flowers, architecture, new faces, clouds, smells, and sounds. We simply have to discipline ourselves to see God in every corner of the world. If we anticipate, God will answer, open, and we will receive.

R.

R-1. My God Doesn't Make Tornadoes

Purpose Statement: *We need to stop blaming God for natural calamities.*

Inevitably, following a natural disaster such as a tornado, earthquake, or flood, some Christian pastor or layperson will make a remark citing God as responsible. They may say, "We don't know why God destroyed that community, but He (sic) must have had some good reason." Such misguided or twisted theology is good reason for the need to have sound religious education. Such statements reflect a more conservative theology. Fundamentalists tend to blame God for terrible destruction and loss of life.
- a. Tornadoes cause theological confusion. They do more than physical damage and destroy lives; they can be seriously misunderstood, theologically. When God is blamed for taking many lives through a natural disaster, some Christians have even abandoned their faith. They say they cannot believe in nor worship such a cruel god. We have all heard of parents who lost a child in a flood or other natural disaster and because they have been raised theologically to believe that God was responsible, they "cursed God" and gave up their faith, exactly what Job's wife told him to do (Job 2:9). Other Christians, less angry or bitter, may only be confused concerning the nature of God and God's love. Who is worse off, the person who believes something unconscionable about God, or the person who becomes angry and gives up the faith?
- b. Tornadoes are not "warnings" or "lessons." If any explanation is ever offered by a well-meaning pastor or other Christian as to why God would do something disastrous, it usually sounds like this:
    1. "God is punishing us for our sins." This means the people who died were very wicked and we survived

because we aren't as sinful or we just haven't gotten ours yet. The truth is we are punished for our sins, not by floods and tornadoes. Punishments may come as heart disease for the sin of not taking care of our bodies or automobile accidents for the sin of not driving carefully. But God had nothing to do with it. It is a cause and effect consequence "built into the nature of life."

Or we may be told,

    2. "This is a warning from God to repent and turn back to God." God does not plan and cause intentional tragedy to teach us lessons. God does not send a tornado and kill a few people to wake the rest of us up. That would be like a parent coaxing their little child's favorite puppy into the street where the neighbor was instructed to run over it with their car to teach the child how dangerous crossing streets can be. Of course, lessons can be gleaned from tragic events, but they were not sent intentionally for such a purpose.

  c. Tornadoes aren't created by God. If God doesn't make tornadoes, who does? God created nature as a part of the world and set it free. Hurricanes, earthquakes, and other natural disasters happen as events in nature and are not inherently evil. They are not bad unless we get in the way. Similarly, God created us and set us free to do what we choose, and this may entail doing evil to others. It is not God doing the evil; it is simply possible in the world. (See sermon C-1, "What On Earth Is God Doing?" for related ideas.)

This fundamentalist theology probably comes from such stories as the flood in Genesis. People misunderstanding God, and God's connection with the disaster, attributed the flood to God. The theology of that age made God responsible for everything. This is inconsistent with the concept of a loving parent-God found in other parts of scripture, primarily the teachings of Jesus. John 9:1-3 tells us God did not punish a man for his sin by causing him to be blind.

See related scripture in the Apocrypha, The Wisdom Of Solomon 1:12-15; 11:17-26.

R-2. In The Name Of God!

Purpose Statement: *Christians have done (and still do) some terrible things and claimed they were done with the approval of God or by God's instructions.*

The message of the previous sermon is that we blame God for tragic events. This message puts a little twist on that theme and suggests we sometimes do terrible things and claim God's sponsorship. Christians have an unfortunate history of violence and wrongdoing in the name of God. The church has hunted down and killed witches, persecuted Jews, owned slaves and justified it, fought needless wars, executed innocent persons, and these are just the glaringly dramatic travesties. History records some ugly events perpetrated by the church and done in the name of God. It still happens today. Many Christians in our country believe God blesses all our wars. Some Christians deny their children medical services and let them die "because it is God's will." Some Christians still believe it is appropriate to discriminate against homosexuals. There are many subtler ways we behave badly as "Christians" and claim God's consent. I believe Gandhi was once asked what was the greatest obstacle to the Christian church in India and he answered, "Christians."

    a. The crime. The crime is involving God in our culpability by claiming God approves, or actually desires, the wrong, foolish, or tragic beliefs or activities in which we engage. An unfortunate and disturbing example is found in 1 Samuel 15:7-33. Samuel slashes King Agag to pieces in front of the altar of God (as an act of worship?) apparently believing this was God's will.

    b. The criminal. While most of us may be guilty some of the time, the most flagrant violators are the "fundamentalists" in each of the three "related" faiths, Christianity, Judaism, and Islam. This is probably true of most, or all, religions. In general, Judaism is an enlightened faith; but the fundamentalist Jews are terribly intolerant and violent. Their activity in the Mideast parallels the early European treatment of the Native Americans in this country. Moslems claim to be loving and peaceable; but viciousness and racism of their fundamentalist sect prejudices outsiders against the faith. While intolerance is found among all Christians, it thrives more among the fundamentalists. It is among the fundamentalists of each religion that we find the most violent, nationalistic, narrow-minded racists and bigots. With the Jews in Jesus' day, it was the Pharisees (Matthew 23) who were the strict keepers of the law. The more conservative we get, the more we attribute to God things that, committed by any one of us, would warrant a prison term. Pastors who tell us the death of the child killed in the car accident was God's will are blaspheming God.

c. The victim. All of us suffer through our misguided understanding of the nature of God. We worship and follow a shadow of God instead God's real presence. We are hurt by such ideas as believing God wants us to go to war instead of negotiating with love and understanding. This unfortunate theology can drive thoughtful people away from the church. Then, there are those who feel the church has discriminated against them.

d. The evidence. The Bible presents some difficult passages that lead to fundamentalist misunderstandings. The church, to justify war and other violence, uses the Old Testament, and God is credited with atrocities as in Joshua 10:11-13 when God rains down hailstones and kills the Amorites. Then God makes the sun stand still so the Israelites would have more time to slaughter their enemies. The New Testament, with but a few exceptions, encourages a much healthier understanding of the nature of God. 1 John 4:7-16 is a fine example of the great love of God espoused by

the New Testament. James 1:12-18 and 5:7-11 attest that God does not do bad things. Matthew 7:9-11 tells how God gives better gifts to us than we, even at our best, could give to each other.
   e. The punishment. We suffer by believing false ideas concerning God and God's will for us, which brings estrangement in our relationship with God, thereby denying the power of God to effect a society of justice and peace.

R-3. An Unidentified Naked Male Running From The Scene

Purpose Statement: *Our regular examination of our relationship with Jesus and the church is probably overdue.*

Various details of the arrest and trial of Jesus are repeated in the four gospels, but only Mark (14:51-52) tells the brief but interesting story of a young man who fled the scene as they tried to arrest him when they arrested Jesus. It is sometimes assumed the man was Mark, because he was young and the incident only appears in the Gospel of Mark. This gospel is purported to be based on the memories of Mark, in whose home Jesus could have met (Acts 12:12) when Mark was a boy. You may well ask, "If this gospel is based on the recollections of Mark, why didn't he identify himself?" Was it because he was embarrassed for having let Jesus down and fleeing, in addition to being rather overexposed?

As a follower of Jesus, what were the young man's emotions as he ran away from danger when Jesus was arrested? He probably felt frightened, disappointed, and confused, as he was naked, cold, and embarrassed. We only have time to examine the first three feelings.
   a. Frightened. It appears that every follower of Jesus ran away in the garden that night. They had ample warning concerning what Jesus was about to face and they certainly didn't want to die. What did Jesus expect of them? Should they stick with him or did he approve of them saving their own lives? Fear of commitment is an expression that is often

associated with thoughts of marriage. Does it resonate with our relationship with the church or with Jesus? Commitment means sacrifice, work, challenge, investment, and even risk. Mark (can we call him that?) was scared for his life. Are we afraid of what commitment will ask of us?

b. Disappointed. The followers of Jesus had unbelievable expectations of Jesus. The four gospels agree on the overwhelming impact Jesus made on, not just his disciples, but also all people. The glorious entry into Jerusalem indicates great anticipation as many accepted him as the Messiah. He would bring them freedom, prosperity, healing, peace, and who knows what else. Then! It was all over. Where were their dreams and hopes? Are there ways in which we find ourselves disappointed in Jesus? If we are honest with his teachings, we have to be disappointed with the lifestyle he advocated: living simply while giving much to the poor, and lovingly turning the other cheek as a reconciler instead of trusting in armaments and physical force, for instance. This turns our disappointment back onto ourselves because, like Mark, occasionally we are running away from taking a stand and facing the commitment.

c. Confused. Followers of Jesus couldn't fully appreciate the dynamics behind the fact that the religious leaders wanted to kill him. They still seemed to be in some doubt as to his method of power (*power* is defined as the ability to accomplish your purpose), which was gentleness and loving persuasion. It has been too easy today for Christians to identify with the church as a fine social organization or club that is well received in our communities. We may find ourselves confused as to what kind of relationship with Jesus is expected by our church in comparison with the demands of Jesus we find in scripture. Consequently, we need to clarify our own expectations.

R-4. Can You Be Trusted With Crayons And Scissors?

Purpose Statement: *How great is the responsibility of being a Christian and are we ready for it?*

Paul used the well-known analogy about the need for some Christians to be fed with milk because they were not yet ready for solid food (1 Corinthians 3:1-2). The writer of Hebrews (who may or may not have been Paul) repeats the analogy in 5:11-14. The implications of these two passages written to the early church is that being a Christian is awesome business requiring wisdom, sensibility, and reliability, among other qualities such as courage and loyalty. It is a responsibility to be taken seriously with an adult-level faith. We must ask ourselves if we are ready for the difficult tasks being a follower of Jesus requires.

Two kindergarteners were on the playground during recess when a large plane flew over. The first child commented on the size of the plane, the engine thrust, and speeds of which the plane was capable. The second child was familiar with the plane's cargo weight limit capacity and how high the plane could fly. Just then, the school bell rang and the first child said, "It's time to go back in and string those dumb beads." Our different roles as Christians require a maturity and capability not to be taken lightly.

    a. Ambassador. As people who call themselves Christians, and professing to follow Christ, we have the automatic responsibility that goes with the position, to be examples of Christ's likeness. Others will judge the Christian faith and our church by how we conduct ourselves. We are the light to the world and the salt of the earth. Will we be good role models or ambassadors?

    b. Diplomat. Can we handle controversy and discuss issues that are divisive? As mentioned in the introduction to this book, one criticism leveled at us pastors is that we preach a very uncomplicated gospel over and over. It is the simple message of, "Turn to God," or "Get yourself saved." Seldom do we get beyond the bare-bones general message: "Be loving and kind." Either we as church members are not ready for the strong stuff, as Paul says, or we as pastors are not ready to serve the solid food — or both. We want to hear the easy, "feel good" messages; but we need to hear the things that may sound offensive. Are we ready for the challenges?

c. Disciple. This word sounds like "discipline," which it certainly requires. Are we still back in the country club environment kind of church with comfortable social functions where the most strenuous chore is deciding what kind of soup and sandwiches to serve at the bazaar? There is nothing wrong with church dinners and choir exchanges; they serve an important function in fellowship. The problem is that we don't often get beyond the polite and easy. Being a Christian requires some serious spiritual exercises, sacrificing some worldly activities, and finding satisfaction in some unpleasant tasks. Are we prepared for the discipline?

d. Martyr. One definition of *martyr* is "a person who chooses to suffer before they would give up their faith." For most of us, an experience of being persecuted for our religious affiliation is rather remote. However, there is another way suffering can test our faith. Are we mature enough to endure serious crises and critical emergencies with the strength of an adult faith? Can we survive a devastating blow, or provide significant support for others going through disaster?

What's on your dinner menu: milk or solid food? Hopefully both.

R-5. Is It Time To Modernize The Gospel?

Purpose Statement: *Are the teachings of Jesus relevant to every age or do they need updating for our modern world situation?*

Can some things be written in stone as the cold hard unchanging fact or does everything become out-dated and need revision to make it relevant and applicable? Everything around us changes.

We have different fashions, technology, laws, entertainment, and an entirely different environment today than we had a few years ago. Even something as critical and revered as the Constitution of the United States had to be changed from what the founding leaders planned. Later, new amendments were added to respect all people, as for example, concerning slavery and voting rights. Prohibition appeared and then disappeared. Yet, we are led to believe if it is in the constitution, it is sacrosanct such as a "questionable" provision for something as useless and destructive as guns. One explanation for the need for change could be that we are not perfect and change is necessary if we are to grow and mature as a civilization. The question being considered is whether or not the gospel (and related to it, the church) needs to change to meet the needs of the modern world.

In the fifth chapter of Matthew, Jesus claims he didn't intend to do away with, or change, the Law of Moses (v. 17), but that he came to fulfill or complete that law. Because Jesus was the more complete revelation of God and God's will for us than anything that preceded him, he necessarily did make changes. It is difficult not to recognize that some of his teachings (vv. 21-48) actually give us an entirely different ethic than previous Old Testament teaching. He repeatedly quotes an Old Testament law and follows with a, "But I tell you," that changes or gives new meaning to the law (vv. 21-22, 27-28, 31-32, 33-34, 38-39, 43-44). Should we expect further updates or changes for today?

    a. Things that should change.
        1. Occasionally, archeology or scholarship research will uncover a new understanding to a biblical word or phrase. This may make a difference in how a certain passage should be worded, which is one of the reasons for ever-more current translations of the Bible. However, these changes are relatively minor.
        2. Certainly there are situations existing today that were unthought of in Jesus' day and where the gospel must be applied to unanticipated circumstances. For example: we must now apply the gospel of love to behavior behind the wheel of an automobile.

3. Our worship services may change to speak to current needs. This is especially true for many hymns we sing. There are so many new hymns with excellent words and theology (I am not referring to the simple repetitive choruses popular today that say very little more than, "Praise the Lord," as beautiful and true as they may be). Some of the old favorite hymns should continue to be used, but occasionally the words should be examined with the congregation to clarify misleading or confusing theology: for example, "God will not let anything bad happen to us," or "We are washed in the blood of the lamb." None of this requires change to the gospel.
4. To reach individuals and meet today's needs may mean new approaches in our witnessing and programming. This, too, has nothing to do with a change in the gospel.

b. Things that never change. As humans we have not changed in our basic needs: the need to be needed, loved, understood, and accepted; the need for God, worship, opportunities to serve, and to be connected with others, are among many possibilities. The basic message of God in the gospel of Jesus is unchanging: we have moral responsibilities, we must think, speak, and act in certain Christian ways, and we must continually find ways to serve our brothers and sisters in love. The message is eternal and unchanging, but our understanding and practice needs focusing.

R-6. The Day That God Changed His Mind

Purpose Statement: *How do we account for the differences in the biblical teachings about God?*

(Yes, I know God cannot be limited by gender, but I had one sermon using a feminine pronoun in B-6, "If God Could

Be Anybody She Wanted To Be, She'd Be Robin Hood" and I needed a balance.)

Many times in scripture, due to an anthropomorphic representation of God, and in an attempt to make the ideas clear and simple, or out of sheer ignorance, we find passages that make God less than God-like. The writer portrays God as very human or far more limited than a god should be. Examples would include: God as violent and cruel, God asking questions God doesn't appear to have the answers to, God "walking in the garden," and (the subject of this sermon) does "God ever have a change of heart?" If God is omniscient, doesn't it seem incongruent to have God change his or her mind concerning what God desires? Examples would include: God wanted the Israelites freed from Egypt and yet kept changing the King of Egypt's mind (i.e. Exodus 10:20). (God using the situation for an opportunity to exercise miraculous displays of power seems implausible.) How about Abraham's getting God to agree to spare Sodom if there were 45 innocent people in the city, then forty, and so on, down to ten (Genesis 18)? Was Abraham able to change God's mind? What about God planning to kill the Israelites for their sin (Exodus 32:1-10) and Moses talking God out of this destruction (vv. 12 and 14)?

Why are there laws and requirements in the Old Testament that are changed in the New Testament? What is a Christian to believe and act upon? In answer to the question, "Did God's mind change?" I suggest four options. God's mind changed because:
- a. God changed. This can't be right because a perfect god would never change and our God is perfect. God is the same and changeless yesterday, today, and forever — that is the nature of God.
- b. The world changed. Has the world really changed morally over the years that it would cause God to require different behavior? Did God want burnt offerings as an act of worship centuries ago, but not now?
- c. We changed. Are people any different today or do we have the same social and personal needs: to be loved, needed, related, and trusted as well as the same sins and problems?

Our basic needs, our general character and who we are as children of God are the same today as they were ages ago.

d. God's mind has not changed. Since the answer has to be, "None of the above," then we must assume the early peoples did not fully understand God and God's will for them. They thought there was some sacred reason why God did not want people to eat pork. Perhaps God never had such a prohibition, they only mistakenly believed it about God. The classic illustration of confusion between God's will in the Old and New Testament periods that still seriously plagues us today is concerning the death penalty. The Old Testament Law requires it and the New Testament teachings of Jesus clearly prohibit it. Yet, concerning this issue so many Christians are clinging to the Old Testament and ignoring Jesus. It is not God who changed, but people who are still growing in their understanding concerning God and God's will for us.

R-7. Touch Me, Turn Me On, And Burn Me Down

Purpose Statement: *What part do, and should, emotions play in our faith experiences?*

We have all been in a variety of church services that run the gamut from the very formal and cold to the other end of the continuum: warm and wild. One Sunday, I attended church where the usher at the door stood rigid pointing with outstretched arm to the head of an aisle where another usher pointed with outstretched arm down the aisle where a third usher waited for us pointing in the same manner to a place in a pew. None of the ushers smiled or spoke. The church could have replaced them with mannequins. They only needed to lower the right arm and lift the left arm when the service ended and we could reverse the process. On more than one occasion I have been in services where there were worshipers running up and down the aisles shouting during the sermon and nurses, complete with nurse uniforms, were present to care for those who swooned in a faint. Is there an acceptable conduct for emotional display in worship? Perhaps the country western song that is plagiarized in the sermon title will provide an outline for discussion.

    a. Experience. We really don't have many examples of individual worship experiences in our Bible. If we include in our definitions of worship the idea that we are *touched* by God, then certainly Paul's conversion experience must be close to the top of the list of dramatic worship moments. Acts 9:1-9 is one of the three times Paul tells of his experiencing the presence of the spirit of Jesus that turned his life around. How many of us who sing, "He Touched Me," can actually attest to the real experience? We have to want it, seek it, and expect it, before it happens to us. At first we may not recognize any anticipation prior to Paul's conversion. Yet, there had to be some serious and emotional spiritual struggle working on him as he observed the love of the Christians he was persecuting. He would have been totally insensitive not to be touched by this experience.

    b. Emotions. No one should argue that worship should *"turn us on"* in a very emotional way. We use two of the body's organs as complimentary symbols of the way we experience and process incoming signals: the brain and the heart. One represents the intellectual response, and the other represents the emotional, or feeling, response. If our faith and our worship experiences are real, they will have both the intellectual and the emotional side. Our experiences must be intellectually respectable, logical, intelligible, and, at the same time, bring evidences that we have connected emotionally: joy, peace, satisfaction, security, hope, and trust. A popular descriptive phrase often used today is, "being spirit filled."

    c. Expression. *"Burn me down"* seems an apt description of Isaiah's being purified with a burning coal in his ultimate worship experience (Isaiah 6:6-7) or Moses' finding God in a burning bush (Exodus 3:1-3) or Jeremiah's burning experience of God's message within him (Jeremiah 20:9).

Jeremiah found he could not refuse to express his emotions and share the word of God. Intellectual activity can be quiet, seemingly cold, and perhaps unobservable. When our emotions are touched, we should notice some expression of excitement or change. How we express those emotions will be a subjective and individual opinion. It may be raising and waving our hand in worship, shouting, just saying "Amen," or "Yes, Jesus," shedding a silent tear, or simply experiencing a joy and warmth inside. It would be inappropriate to identify one pattern of expression — such as speaking in tongues — as the true evidence of the presence of the Spirit of God in us. Each of us is different and will answer to different experiences and expressions. No matter how the expression is made, it must inevitably bear fruit in our lives.

R-8. Becoming A Tricky Old Dog

Purpose Statement: *It is never too late for us to grow and change.*

The old adage, "You can't teach an old dog new tricks," contrary to the wisdom in most proverbial statements, is almost dead wrong. We can learn, change, renew, refresh, grow, and continue to mature mentally and spiritually much further into old age than we have been led to think. Another old adage, closer to the truth, claims we can never stand still; we either progress or regress. Stagnation is decay. If we are not improving, we are definitely losing ground. This seems like an important subject for Christians to consider. Let's examine the matter.

    a. What? We mustn't give up as we grow a little older, and we certainly shouldn't use our age as an excuse. Now that I have reached my sixties I have found it very convenient to blame my lapses of memory and just plain carelessness on aging. Forgetting names or things to do used to be embarrassing. Now, I just say, "I'm getting old." It works, unfortunately. And it is wrong. We are capable of more than the sneaky, lazy side of our nature cares to admit. Adam and Eve had children when they were over 100 years old. Noah's children were born when he was over 500 years old. We presume Mrs. Noah was a comparable age. Together they built an ark and endured a flood at age 600. Moses spent the years between his eightieth and 120th birthdays leading a complaining mob through a terrible desert. Granted, these numbers are more symbolic and are not comparable with our calendar years today; yet, they could well represent activities at a more mature age. Genesis 21:1-7 tells us Isaac was born when Abraham was 100 years old and Sarah in the same chronological ballpark. If those figures are unrealistic, look up the ages at which many of the great thinkers, inventors, composers, explorers, scientists, and others did their memorable work.

b. How? How does this apply to the Christian or church member? Don't stop learning, studying, and growing spiritually or mentally. Learn new hymns. Engage in ongoing Christian education classes. Go with new patterns of private and corporate worship. Spend even more time in serious Bible study with sound resources for aids. Volunteer for new tasks to challenge yourself. Do something you have never ventured in before, such as calling door to door, working in a soup kitchen, ringing Christmas bells for the Salvation Army, and the like. Write a book, a pamphlet, your memoirs, or a religious play.

c. Why? We will be much healthier mentally, physically, and spiritually for our continued activity and new adventures. Studies are showing us, for example, that the onset of Alzheimer's disease is forestalled as we continue to grow and use our minds. This may be true for other ailments such as Parkinson's disease. By learning new things and maintaining a program of mental and physical activity, we will also be sharper spiritually. We will grow in our relationship with God. Life will be far more interesting and even exciting. We will enjoy life so much more. Our lives will be so much more productive. It is a common mistake we often make to consider the elderly the church of yesterday, and the children the church of tomorrow. The elderly and children are the church of today. Use it or lose it, they tell us; and they are right.

R-9. How Vulgar Can We Be?

Purpose Statement: *What are the limits of acceptable vulgarity for the Christian?*

Is it "zero tolerance"? Or does being "down to earth," "only human," or "one of the good old boys (girls)" give us permission for a certain amount of crudity, within limits? What are we discussing? The vulgarity would include, for example, cursing (there seems to be a progression from darn to damn to ...) and telling, or tolerating, crude jokes concerning sex, racism, or other subjects either of a "delicate" nature, or told in an inappropriate manner.

    a. Temptation. There is pressure from certain circles to "join the crowd" by using the language, telling the kind of stories, or showing your condonation with laughter. There is an image to maintain to be "one of the boys." Refraining from exhibiting crude behavior and language quickly can identify you as prudish. You can easily be ridiculed as a "goody-goody" and find yourself not fitting in with the crowd if you don't seem to enjoy crudity, and certainly if you object. If we have friends of that persuasion, the temptation to join in is very strong.

    b. Sensation. Where do we draw the line between what is acceptable and what isn't? Television struggles with this issue constantly (or maybe it doesn't). The use of certain words and situations — noticeably sexual — become progressively more daring and permissive. This lends an aura of acceptance and commonality, the message being, "Everyone is doing it." There is a strong contrast between the language heard in the schools of today and when I was in high school. When my generation was in high school, only males used bad language and told off-color stories, and then never around adults or females. Today, the halls of high schools are blue with a constant stream of vulgar expletives regardless of who is present. Comic pages are the most considerate of our senses, they only use #@%&! to denote crude language — so far. T-shirts and bumper stickers are not so thoughtful of our feelings. People walk around with shirts decorated with slogans and comments too crude for words. The things suggested would have been unimaginable a few years ago. Often the expressions will be worded such as to create a double-entendre. One interpretation appears innocent. But, if you are aware of the other secondary risqué meaning, then the evil mind is yours! You have the problem, not them. The perpetrator can then feel cute and amused over an insult to you, and our children are exposed to it all.

c. Explanation. Why is it all so objectionable? Where do we draw the lines? James 3:1-12 explains how our language offends others, as well as how it indicates the kind of person we are (particularly v. 12). The same mouth curses and swears, and also praises God (vv. 9-11); though that last part may be giving the crude person the benefit of the doubt. What we say can hurt others, offend, influence, and create an unsavory atmosphere. Romans 3:14 criticizes us for crude speech. Jesus (Matthew 15:10-20) tells us that it is not what we eat (they were worried about eating food offered to idols) that makes us unclean, but it is things we say (v. 18) that come from the heart that indicate the kind of person we really are. Jesus says this is what makes us unclean (v. 20). Jesus repeats this idea in Matthew 12:33-35 and goes on to a frightening prospect by saying that we shall be held accountable for every crude and idle word we utter (vv. 36-37). It all has to do with respect for others, dignity, and tastefulness. Anything that is useless and offends others is totally inappropriate. Paul says we should fill our minds with what is pure, noble, honorable, and such, in a beautiful passage from Philippians (4:8).

R-10. When Christianity Becomes A Waste Of Time

Purpose Statement: *Good Christian stewardship demands an efficient use of our time and talents.*

So many of the stories of Jesus have interesting little twists to them that strike us as strange, unless we get so familiar with the stories as to render them common and not out of the ordinary. One such story is about Jesus sending out his followers to preach and heal (Mark 6:7-13). There are interesting elements to explain such as the instruction not to take anything, but the one that always intrigued me was that they were not to persist or pressure their listeners. Unlike some telemarketers or door-to-door religious folks who find "No" an unintelligible answer, Jesus seemed to suggest the disciples should move on if there is no initial response in the town. "Shake the dust from your feet and move on to the next town" (Matthew 10:14). My first reaction was: "Jesus, I think you are wrong. We should linger and be more persuasive. Keep trying; after all, these folks are important and need saving." But Jesus had another agenda: we must not waste energy and time. There is only so much we can do when the "harvest is too great for the number of workers" (Luke 10:2). Efficiency is a key stewardship idea.

    a. Efficiency in church. As Ecclesiastes 3 reminds us, there is a time to stick to it and a time to give up. Every Christian must evaluate what she or he is doing in the church. Is what we are doing the best use of our talents or more of a waste of our Christian time? Can someone else do this job more effectively, and do we belong in another slot? Conservation of energy is all the rage today and rightly so. We must apply the same criteria and organization to the conservation of our personal energy. Spend it where it is the most effective; where it will do the most good. Be careful: this efficiency evaluation is not to be used as an excuse to avoid unpleasant responsibilities.

    b. Efficiency in social action. First, every Christian should find areas of social concern where they can invest themselves in issues that will make better communities, or bring peace and justice. However, this is a difficult area to analyze in terms of efficient Christian service. We need to feel that our efforts are amounting to something. Social action becomes extremely disappointing or depressing when we expend so much time and energy with so little results. If we are unable to realize some tangible change or sense that we have made an impact, discouragement will sap our strength. We can "shake the dust from our shoes" and move on in two different ways: either we change our tactics or we change our activity. If the goal of the social action we're involved in is relatively unattainable or impractical, we change the focus, or change the approach. Instead of standing on the corner with a protest poster, it may be time to give that up and spend the time contacting legislators. Or, after a while, it may be time to find a new cause for our energies.

c. Efficiency in all things. Someone has said that we "should not waste time, it is what life is made of." We need to prioritize our lives, putting "first things first." Examine your daily schedule to see how the time is spent. Is it in activities that serve some good purpose that is constructive, restful and renewing, helpful, enjoyable, or meaningful? We could find we are wasting time on things that are harmful, useless, and entirely unenjoyable. Life is too short and time too valuable. John Wesley, the co-founder of the United Methodist Church, advises us never to spend any more time in any place than is necessary. Methodists "... pick(ed) up the very fragments of.... Time, that not a moment might be lost." We must invest ourselves in productive and helpful ways. Certainly, enjoyment is important and needs to be one of the criteria. My wife asks me, "You don't like coffee; why do you drink it?" I say, "I don't know." Our common complaint is there "isn't enough time in the day to do everything." And yet, most of us haven't sharpened and focused our priorities. We are wasting time and life.

S.

S-1. When Worlds Collide: Sacred And Secular

Purpose Statement: *How does our faith relate to the rest of our lives, including the interaction between religious and civic responsibilities?*

    I have a friend who is a very conservative minister espousing the typical conservative theology such as: everything that happens is planned by God for a purpose that we don't always understand, or people who don't profess Jesus as their Savior are condemned to eternal hell, and other such delights. Strange as it may seem, he is very liberal in his politics and positions on social issues. You ask how this can be? Perhaps, liberal politics and conservative theology fit together just fine and I simply don't understand. But if the two positions are really somewhat mutually exclusive, there may be a very reasonable explanation as to how someone could maintain both positions and see no incongruity.

    a. We compartmentalize our worlds. Perhaps we could say that we live in two worlds: one sacred and the other secular. We can go to church and do our religious duties in the world of incense and candles, then step out the door into the "real" world where religion doesn't belong or work. We have conveniently kept these two worlds separate in order to minimize any conflicts. Jesus shared some thoughts concerning the conflicts between these two worlds. The Pharisees tried to trap Jesus with questions concerning paying taxes to Rome, and he responded by taking a coin and indicating we pay allegiance to the governing authorities to whom it is due and to God where it is due (Matthew 22:15-21). It isn't recorded for our edification, but I like to think he took time to explain how the two were related. He dwelt at some length (John 17:9-19) on these two worlds and the need for us to know our appropriate relationship to each. The truth is we live in two worlds but should not keep them separate. While we have civic responsibilities, our religious loyalties always take precedence. We always obey God's will as our faith world dictates, and follow civic law only when it does not conflict with God's law. When we understand that, our faith will guide us through every aspect of our lives by putting a sacred tone to everything secular. The entire universe is God's and we relate to the world by superimposing the sacred essence over it to indicate how the world should be if we were all to act appropriately. Currently, too many of us do not allow our sacred world to speak to the secular world as if our religion were irrelevant to the secular world. Take a page out of Amos and see how he castigated the Hebrews for not allowing their religion to govern their daily business relationships. The results were greed and opulence for some at the expense of poverty and injustice for others, and that was in the days when the religious law *was* the civil law.

b. Or we merge our worlds. Either, as in the first point, we live in two separate unrelated worlds, or sometimes the two worlds become tangled in an unholy alliance that corrupts both. There have been ample historic illustrations of church and state fraternizing too much. England provides a fine example of the church and state becoming too dependent upon each other so that special privileges and inappropriate influence have corrupted both worlds. The church crowned heads of state, and the clergy received their "living" through state appointments. Who you know determines who gets what. In our country, there are strong pressures from the Christian right to make our nation and government "Christian" by taking advantage of our majority to attain positions of special privilege such as: "in God we trust," "one nation under God," Bible reading and prayer (Christian prayer) in the schools, and so forth. If you are Buddhist, atheist, or any other non-Christian "you don't have to participate!" (see message C-10, "Why Teachers Can't Pray"). When the Christian church becomes special friends with the state, we give up our privilege of standing apart to speak a prophetic word to the secular.

We compromise our position and become too secular at the cost of the sacred. To be fair, we must acknowledge Paul's comments (Romans 13:1-7) concerning Christians obeying the governing authorities because God appoints them. Paul would be the first to say that when those state authorities are in opposition to God's law, we need to obey God first and unquestionably. That is what Paul himself did. Paul's idea that "our government is appointed by God" only means God wants us to have orderliness in our society to maintain peace and justice.

S-2. Imagine That!

Purpose Statement: *Allow some exciting creativity into your faith world.*

One of the most imaginative events in the ministry of Jesus was the time (Mark 2:1-12) some men brought a friend to Jesus to be healed. There was such a crowd gathered around Jesus they could not get near. Undaunted, they used their imagination and broke a hole in the roof (to the chagrin of the homeowner) and lowered the man down to Jesus. That is exactly what we need in our spiritual life, a creative imagination. Things go stale occasionally and need revitalization. For example:
   a. Church worship. This may be a bad example; some of us may have gone overboard occasionally with some of the colorful activities used today to enliven our worship services (see message P-7, "Should Acolytes Wear Sneakers?"). I am not a fan of "clowning" and some of the other non-traditional ways of spicing up worship today, but their heart is in the right place. While putting "new wine in old wine skins" can be disastrous, a little new grape juice somewhere appropriate can be very renewing. It is more than learning new hymns, but this is a good example to start with. There are some exciting new songs being used in our churches today: "God Of The Sparrow," "Lord, You Have

Come To The Lakeshore," "We Are The Church," or "Hymn Of Promise." By changing the worship order, and adding new things tastefully, it can bring new life.
  b. Personal worship. Try a new location. Try new resources, even ones you may not agree with. Simply ask yourself why you are even doing this. A sharper focus will lead to fresh adventures.
  c. Church tasks. If you are placed on a committee, given a special task, or any kind of responsibility in the church life, use your imagination and be creative. First, read up on what's available for help and what is being done elsewhere. Then ignore the *sacred rule* that insists, "It has always been done this way." There are many overlooked opportunities for putting new life into old activities or creating new ministries.
  d. Serving others. No doubt just being reminded that we have a responsibility to help other people is a giant step. Look around and see who is hurting, left out, or new that we haven't greeted or even noticed before. Try to imagine exciting and interesting ways of ministering to our neighbors and community. Remember when someone came up with a startling new thought and you kicked yourself saying, "I could have thought of that"?

Be creative!

S-3. You Thought It Couldn't Get Any Worse

Purpose Statement: *How to deal with depression.*

Everyone deals with depression at one time or another: things go bad, we get too little sunshine in the winter season, or for no apparent reason at all, and we become blue or down in the dumps. Then there are severe cases of depression of a crisis nature where expert help is necessary. Each one of us could use some clues or secrets in how to deal with depression — others and ours. This message will acknowledge and skip over the obvious ways of seeking help by going to God in worship and prayer, and instead will focus on other secondary, albeit helpful, ways to conquer depression. First, which three Bible personalities whose names begin with *J* became depressed for very good reasons? Jesus wept over the city of Jerusalem and on another occasion must have been terribly discouraged when he suffered the ordeal in Gethsemane garden, a mock trial, and the cross. Job was so depressed even his friends couldn't cheer him up. Jeremiah hit rock bottom. Jeremiah 20:7-18 is a powerful poem commemorating Jeremiah's devastation because of the ordeal he faced as a prophet for God. He is mocked and friendless, and curses the day he was born (vv. 14-18). The people tormented and persecuted him because he dared to preach God's message (vv. 8 and 10). It becomes impossible not to say what God wants him to say; holding it in causes it to burn like a fire (v. 9). God was on his side (v. 11) and finally he is able to sing praises to God (v. 13). Some secrets in defeating depression might include:

    a. Accomplishing something. We can conquer depression appreciably if we become busy with some worthwhile task, or if we have successfully achieved some of our goals. To feel that we have made a difference in our world will usually lift our spirits considerably. Find something in the church that needs fixing, donate blood, write your legislator concerning an issue, or create something. Set some goals and get busy; sweat equity is part of God's plan. Jeremiah (7:1-7) was given an important task. God has more job openings than you and I can begin to fill.

    b. Serving others. Take a hot meal to a shut-in, phone a lonely person, be alert to opportunities when out in public to share a kind word or pleasant moment's conversation, or find a way to let another know you love them. Just remembering, "there are many people who are worse off than we are" is not the tonic to cheer us up; we must actively do something about it. Focus on showing love to others and alleviating some of their sufferings, and we will find ourselves healed. Be careful this does not become the reason for your altruism; self-interest is not healing the way true concern for others is. Job was *too* preoccupied with self.

c. Planning ahead. God prepared Jeremiah very early on for his ministry (1:4-8). Jeremiah could work his way through his troubles because he had developed a sustaining relationship with God. In situations — overcoming grief, meeting temptations, and struggling with depression — we must not wait until the need arises before we begin the remedy. If we turn to prayer, find meaningful tasks, help others in need, or simply find ways to love others, we begin our healing process even before our healing is ever needed. We begin to fight depression before we ever become depressed and it will not only prepare us for dealing with depression when it strikes, but will be efficacious for keeping depression from ever knocking on our door.

S-4. Some Things You Don't Want To Know

Purpose Statement: *Knowledge brings responsibility.*

"What you don't know won't hurt you" is an interesting idea to ponder. The refutation I have always heard is, "like a tack on a chair." But in one sense, when it hurts you, you could say that you now "know it." There is the rumor about you that is being passed around. The rumor isn't true, and you don't know about it, and may never know about it. Even though you may never realize how it has hurt you, it in fact is hurting you. In a related way, there is the theological issue of knowledge and responsibility. Can we be held responsible for things of which we are ignorant? Remember the Garden of Eden situation, where Eve and Adam were instructed not to eat of the tree of knowledge and when they did, they then knew right and wrong and suffered the consequences for their disobedience (Genesis 3:1-13, 22-24)? Are there things you do not want to know? Let us consider three.

a. The more you comprehend the rules, the more responsible you will be for obeying the rules. The Catholic church used to have a policy that if you were a non-Catholic and unfamiliar with the catechism or the beliefs of the Catholic church there was still a chance you could be saved. However, if once you became familiar with the doctrine of the Catholic church, and then did not accept Christ and join the church, you were lost. It all hinged on how much you knew and in certain situations you were better off not knowing. The basic philosophy behind this thinking has merit. If you eliminate the salvation part and perhaps the implication, there may only be one true church. After all, Jesus expressed the same thought in John 15:22 when he said we did not understand sin until he came and now we no longer have the excuse of ignorance. If I understand civil law, we are held culpable for knowing the highway regulations of a state we are traveling in but may not live in. We cannot plead ignorance. If we don't know the laws of that state, we need to get off the road or get out of the state. Can we plead ignorance of God's rules and not be held responsible?

b. The more you know about injustice, the more responsible you will be for serving others. There is a powerful sermon idea, F-9, "Out Of Sight; Out Of Mind: The Ostrich Approach To World Hunger," in the first book. We think that it helps alleviate our troubled conscience if we aren't very much aware of the hunger and suffering going on around us in the world. If the plight of starving children in Bangladesh is vividly portrayed before us on our television screens or in an especially poignant sermon, we feel disturbed and moved to respond. Can many of us honestly say concerning the suffering in the world, "I didn't know?" It is the mandate of every responsible Christian to become informed concerning our social and political world situations through assiduous study. We have some awareness; now we must get the full facts.

c. The more sensitive you become the more you will hurt. Ecclesiastes 1:18 tells us the wiser we become the more we will worry and the more we know the more it will hurt.

To be like Jesus, or grow in God's love, is to become more sensitive to the pain of others. The suffering and injustice in the world will seem intolerable. Serving others and doing much to alleviate suffering around us will assuage some, but not all, of the pain. Being sensitive necessitates loving and caring and hurting when others hurt. Just as Jesus wept over Jerusalem, we weep with those who weep. Psychologists tell us we must have "empathy" in place of "sympathy": the latter is to "feel" the pain of others, while the former is supposed to be caring without so much "feeling." However, the dictionary doesn't differentiate that clearly between the two ideas. If we don't feel disturbed over the suffering of others, we aren't sensitive or loving enough. Nevertheless, the point is we mustn't let so much tragedy in our world spoil our lives or destroy our peace of mind and our appreciation of beauty, joy, and love. There is a time (Ecclesiastes, again) for joy and celebration, and a time for weeping and commiseration. The secret is a healthy and wholesome balance.

Facetiousness aside, of course, we want to be cognizant of these things. The more we know, the more responsible person we can become: thus the greater our integrity, the more extensive our service to others, and the more generous our love.

S-5. Lions And Cows Dining Together: Seeing Is Believing

Purpose Statement: *We must have a vision that peace is realistically attainable.*

One of my first sermons in my home church as a college student was on pacifism. One of my Sunday school teachers who taught me that Jesus preached pacifism (though she did not know she was teaching me those ideas) came to me after the sermon and said, "That was such a wonderful sermon; too bad it won't work." It is an understatement to say the world desperately needs peace today. As I write this, our president is trying to get the support of people of our country and other countries concerning the war with Iraq. The mockery is that we were already at war with Iraq and we bombed them regularly. Our world is filled with death and destruction. On the domestic scene, our country is one of most violent in the world. More than most any other country in the world we have a larger percentage of our citizens behind bars. We simply don't know how to make peace at home or abroad. We think the vision of the "peaceable kingdom" in Isaiah 65:17-25 is "nice," but impractical ("too bad it won't work"), even though it represents God's will for our world and Jesus taught us how to achieve it. Matthew 5:9 tells us how important peacemakers are, while Romans 12:9-21 reveals the secret of attaining peace. Yet very few believe it will work. It is our only solution since nothing else has worked. When will we learn that God's way does work?

    a. Understand it. Read the many historic instances (concerning which most of us are ignorant) where God's way of peace has succeeded, even under highly improbable circumstances. There are dramatic examples of pacifist victories in wartime, under cruel dictators, as well as many examples of the success of love in personal confrontations. One very good source among many would be, *Victories Without Violence*, by A. Ruth Fry. She gives countless examples of wonderful reconciliations in dangerous situations. Turning the other cheek and loving an enemy has a great historic track record unbeknownst to most people. It works. We must become better informed.

    b. Believe it. It seems strange that we pay lip service to Jesus and his teachings and still believe what he taught is impractical. It should seem natural and obvious that God would provide a way for individuals and nations to live in peace and make peace without violence. We are brainwashed to be forceful, dominant, aggressive, tough, mean, hard, unforgiving, and selfish. Anything less than this posture is seen as weak and cowardly. Consequently, we don't believe that enemies are human, nor will they respond to peace and love. It is a truism that we have to "dehumanize" our enemies so that we can excuse our killing. They are God's children, too, and, believe it or not, like us, have a spark of divinity in them.

c. Meditate on it. Setting our minds on peace, and peaceable ways, has to become a serious part of our worship and prayer. As trite as it may seem to say it, it is a powerful truth that we must have a vision of peace, a vision of sitting down with our enemies, whether it be another "evil axis" nation or the angry neighbor living next door, and begin to share together and listen, in love. Imagine, dream, and pray about the possibilities. I really believe the vision is missing. We don't believe it is possible because we haven't "seen" the vision.

d. Practice it. It starts with each individual. "Let there be peace on earth, and let it begin with me," is a hymn we sing and think we mean. When a neighbor or motorist gets angry, it is a wonderful opportunity for us to show love! When did you last write our national leaders to urge peaceful solutions or for our country not to attack, or bomb, another country? Get up each morning and tell yourself, "I will be loving like Jesus today and be a peacemaker." Then write your senator.

S-6. Analysis Of A Saloon

Purpose Statement: *Do churches and taverns offer the same services, and does our church do a better job of it?*

One Saturday night, a nightclub burned to the ground, but the resident parrot escaped through the window and flew across the street and into a church. The next morning, Sunday, the parrot awoke during the morning service and looked around confused. The parrot, remembering the fire, but not his trip across the street, thought, "Wow, they redecorated this bar in a hurry." Noticing the minister serving communion the parrot commented, "And they have hired a new bartender." Seeing the choir elicited the response, "I see they have a whole new floor show." As the parrot looked out over the congregation, it noted, "But, I see it's the same old crowd."

What attracts people to taverns? We read in the newspapers about the fights that break out in bars and outside of bars. We seldom hear of that happening at family restaurants, fast food chains, or churches. What goes on in bars and why? There are reasons why we do something or go someplace, and it might be helpful to ask what individuals are looking for that sends them to bars. In that connection we should ask why people go to church and what they are *really* looking for at church. Remember the parable of the dinner party where the guests didn't come (Luke 14:15-24)? Jesus implied that we take the good news to the poor and "unfortunate." We must not read too much into the story and think it means that the church members (the first invitees?) didn't respond (although that is certainly another sermon topic substantiated by other scriptures: Matthew 7:21-23; Matthew 21:28-32; Luke 18:9-14; and others). On the other hand, be wary of practicing paternalism.

    a. How is a tavern like a church? There are at least three reasons why folks go to a bar.
        1. They are in need of fellowship, and sometimes they find it there.
        2. They have problems and the bartender (according to myth perpetuated by television and movies) will listen sympathetically, as may other of the denizens.
        3. Another objective may be the seeking of an image for oneself.

First, our desire for fellowship is acknowledged as a common, if not universal, need. We need socialization to be healthy individuals and will seek out friendship in all kinds of places. Second, suggesting the problems people have sends them to bars searching for answers is not hard to understand; drink is a popular opiate with which to drown our frustrations. And, finally, one of the major motivators for many is the need to create an image for themselves that will be acceptable to some group. A beer baron once said of his brew, "The customer imbibes the image." (*Hot War on the Consumer*, David Sanford, editor, p. 14.) Whether it is a tavern, a nightclub or a "sophisticated" private wine gathering, one element is common: the desire to impress a certain clientele that we are cool, daring, rugged individuals; that we are sophisticated or any of a number of other roles we want to play. What about church? We go to church for similar reasons: for fellowship (with God and others), because it helps us with problems or gives directions to our lives, and perhaps to create for ourselves the image of a kind and good person. (Note: contrary to our stereotypes, we will find some very loving and caring people in taverns, as well as some mean spirited folks in church.)

WIZARD OF ID

By permission of John L. Hart FLP, and Creators Syndicate, Inc.

  b. How is a church not like a tavern?
1. The fellowship should be deeper and more meaningful at church than at a bar, though this isn't always necessarily true. You and I will determine the reality.
2. As for our problems, the church offers far more than the "escape" a bar provides. Christians care enough to make sacrifices for others, and hopefully offer a sincere non-judgmental love in caring for a multitude of problems.
3. Finally, the church tells us that we don't need an "image" or persona. We are acceptable for who we really are and loved despite any peculiarities. God loves us and we love one another. Without "putting on airs" that love helps us grow naturally into God's grace and fulfill our potential.

c. How do we take the church to the tavern? Tavern folks aren't in the tavern all of the time. They are our neighbors, co-workers, and the stranger we meet almost anywhere (and some of them are already in church). One of our unfortunate tendencies is to proselytize those who go to church elsewhere. We encourage folks to change churches instead of reaching out to the unchurched. For some Christians, it may mean a ministry actually taken to the bars. (Please don't drink the water.) People who frequent bars and nightclubs are looking for the church and don't know it. They are not going to believe it if we tell them. It calls for establishing some very trusting and caring relationships. The fields are ripe for harvest, and so are the saloons, for the more courageous and creative evangelists among us (Matthew 9:35-38). To accept this mission, Jesus says, we will be like lambs going out among the wolves (Luke 10:1-3).

S-7. Get Over It!

Purpose Statement: *We have to learn how to really forgive and accept forgiveness. This includes forgiving ourselves.*

Of course, one of the basic tenets of the Christian faith is forgiveness. Everyone knows that, but not enough of us know how to forgive ourselves, others, and how to accept the forgiveness of others. The first thing Jesus does after teaching his followers the Lord's Prayer is to elaborate on one of the main ideas: forgiveness (Matthew 6:14-15). We have to forgive in order to be forgiven. Later (Matthew 18:21-35), Jesus shares a parable that dramatizes this subject, after he has responded to Peter's question about how many times we are to forgive offensive behavior. The number "seventy times seven" means indefinitely, as we all know. Reiterating these ideas Sirach 28:1-7 (another chance to use the Apocrypha if you are so inclined) also adds perceptive thoughts regarding hate and our neighbor's faults. Forgiveness is one of those topics we are so familiar with, and yet we need to hear more often.

a. Forgive. A major hurdle to forgiveness may be the enjoyment we experience when we have "something on somebody." One of those self help books might have identified this posture as one of the games we play: "I've got you now, you *#@&#." We can actually revel in "being hurt or offended." It is another form of martyrdom: "Look how I am a victim, sorely abused. You did this to me, that makes you a bad person and you owe me." Secretly, we may be delighted when someone offends us (perhaps this should be an entire sermon in itself). There is much to be said concerning forgiving. How dare we expect to ever be forgiven unless we forgive. When Jesus said, "Let the one who hasn't sinned cast the first stone," he humbles us.
b. Reconcile. Do we really believe that forgiveness is just saying the magic words, "I forgive you?" It means much more: we must repair the relationship, work out the differences, and actually love each other. Without the rest of this, forgiveness never happens. It may even mean reparations. And, it often will mean admitting we were also probably at fault ourselves.
c. Accept forgiveness. In many cases, it may be easier to accept forgiveness than to grant it, as Jesus suggested in the parable cited above. The exception is the special case when we won't accept God's absolution because we won't forgive ourselves. Our remorse becomes so great that we either wallow in self-pity, or simply think our sin was so great we do not deserve to be pardoned. There are acts so heinous we ask, "How can they live with themselves?" And if we feel that way concerning our own sin, we can be severely condemning of our self on occasions. We need to believe Jesus when he said God *does* forgive us and we must accept God's mercy by receiving that pardon. Jesus said there was only one unforgivable sin, blasphemy against the Holy Spirit (Matthew 12:31-32); which may be interpreted as *simply not accepting God's forgiveness.*
d. Change. In order that we might truly be forgiven, it is imperative we give up the sin we are asking pardon for, or that we eliminate the offensive activity or attitude.

e. Forget it! Get over it! Let it go; never dredge up bygone altercations or alienations. In marriages it is easy to let the heat of a current argument tempt us to resurrect some past difference, hurt, or offense with which to remind the other party, "Remember that bad thing you did?" If we cannot forget it and get over it, it was never forgiven.

S-8. Three Little Pigs — Jesus' Version

Purpose Statement: *Sometimes we have to preach the obvious such as: we need a strong faith foundation when trials come.*

Jesus was right, you know. There was only need for two little pigs; the third one is redundant. One little pig built a house of straw and another built a house of twigs, but the fate was the same for both: the bad wolf blew both houses down. A third pig built with bricks and survived. Jesus only has two little pigs. One builds on a strong foundation, the rock. The other builds on a weak foundation, the sand. The bad wolf came and blew the house built on sand down with the help of flood waters (Matthew 7:24-27). The message of this subject is an example of the universal sermon. As one homiletics professor put it, "We only have one sermon to preach, we just change the title and a few illustrations." Obvious as it is, the truth is still vital and needs an outing every so often. There seem to be three elements to the three (or two) little pigs story.

a. One wise and one foolish little pig. God did a dangerous thing by turning us loose on our own in a world full of bad wolves. We have been given a brain and God is counting on our using it like a wise little pig and not like a foolish little pig. Analogous to Eve and Adam, we are given free will to make critical choices. We are on our own. The decisions we make will determine much of our fate.

b. One good and one bad foundation. This is an example where we probably know what to do, but for some reason we don't do it. We know eating junk food, and lots of it, is detrimental to our health, yet we persist. Likewise, we believe Jesus knows best for us, but like the rebellious teenager we are determined to do our own thing. When given a choice of building a strong faith that answers life's critical questions, gives us a moral compass and enriches our life and all our relationships; or the alternative of sand castles, we choose the latter. The good foundation is the teachings of Jesus. The bad foundation is our own devices, as we think we can go it alone without God. We have a home, insurance, a job, retirement, (perhaps even a gun) and so forth. What else could we possibly need?

c. The bad wolf. Our problem may be that we don't believe in the bad wolf. Those trials and tribulations that we read about in the papers can't happen to us. We are special. Surely God wouldn't permit those accidents and calamities to happen to us. Yet, Jesus predicted that his followers would suffer, and the Bible makes it very clear that bad things do happen to good people. Once the bad wolf comes knocking, it may be far too late to start your construction. Selection of a good foundation must come early in the process. You cannot purchase bad wolf insurance when she is sitting in your living room sharpening her teeth.

S-9. Can Pagan Objects Be Sanitized?

Purpose Statement: *Are there certain objects or ideas that are off limits to Christians because they have been contaminated by pagan or wicked associations in the past?*

A good illustration of this concern is Halloween. When it rolls around each year, there will be the inevitable conversation by some Christians saying the holiday is fraught with paganism, associated with devil worship, and is consequently a bad influence on our children, perhaps even on our adults. The early church had to deal with this problem and Paul spoke on occasions concerning eating food that had been prepared for idol worship (1 Corinthians 10:18-33). The church was continually threatened by religions with superstitious, wicked, and harmful practices. Our comparable enemies today are the idolizing of materialism, glamour, sex, wealth, and excessive entertainment to name a few of the more obvious. Then, Paul discussed food intended for idol worship; today Paul would have to discuss something such as a concern over Halloween and associations with the occult or "spooky." This would include witches in children's books, devils for team mascots, the number 666, and Harry Potter books, to name a few. Right-wing Christians attacked Procter and Gamble believing that P & G's logo was filled with pagan symbols. Their attack was successful enough to cost the company some serious financial loss. In another case, one well-known Christian denomination had to suspend one of its pastors for worshiping with pagans in an interfaith service at Yankee Stadium for the families killed in the attack on the World Trade Towers. Christmas is suspect because it has borrowed carelessly in its origins: the day chosen was originally a pagan holiday and even the Christmas tree may be tainted. Next, we may have to give up the names of the days of our week for their pagan association: Wednesday or Thursday, for example.

   a. For most Christians, everything is inherently clean. Acts 10:1-33 (particularly vv. 9-15) is commonly used to excuse us from some Old Testament regulations such as what we may eat and our associations with ritually unclean persons. It is the story of Peter being shown animals in a large sheet let down from heaven. The key verse says everything is clean that God has declared clean (v. 15). The Genesis creation story tells us that God thought all of creation was good. Occasionally, we are able to make "clean" what people earlier made "unclean." For example, we sing great hymns to tunes that began their musical career as bawdy tavern songs. We (with the help of Jesus) took an object of the worst possible kind — the cross — and turned it into a focal center of worship.

Everything is "good" unless ...

b.   ... it is harmful. In the 1 Corinthians 10 passage, everything is good unless there is obvious harm (v. 23). Poison may be good for some things, but not very helpful if we drink it in excess. Cars are terribly convenient, but they may become death instruments when we use them wrongly. Tornadoes are not wicked as long as we stay out of their way.

c.   ... it is used in a pagan way. Something that is perfectly acceptable becomes inappropriate when used for evil purposes. Could sex be an illustration of this? Paul said not to participate in pagan practices (v. 20).

d.   ... it leads others astray. The major concern in the Corinthians passage is that you should not eat what will mislead or confuse others (vv. 25-33). It will not hurt you to eat food prepared for idols, but you should choose to abstain when others who are present may not understand or may be led into compromise themselves. This is reinforced by the passage in Romans 14:13-23 where Paul says that we are free to eat anything, however, we should abstain from anything that will hurt a sister or brother (vv. 20-21). There are limits to this. We must use common sense; if we abstained from everything because it offended or misled someone, we would not use blood transfusions, or any other medical resources for that matter. There is a time to sympathize and there is a time to lead and make a witness.

Conclusion: We have sanitized Halloween (which comes from a Christian holiday, All Hallows' Eve and All Saints' Day) for Christian use. It is a healthy thing that children have conquered the "demons" with witch and devil costumes. It is tantamount to thumbing their noses at superstition. Also with mascots such as Eureka College Red Devils and Duke Blue Devils. Unless they are excessively violent, witch, and wizard stories are handled quite well by children, until superstitious adults contaminate them. Looking for Satanism in symbolism, numbers (666), and logos is nothing more than an immature witch-hunt.

S-10. A Just-In-Case Arrangement With God

Purpose Statement: *It may not be possible to have a playing-it-safe kind of approach to religion.*

Judges 6 tells the story of Gideon testing God (or an angel of God) just to be sure he was talking to the right person. Gideon devises two schemes involving a burnt offering (vv. 17-22) and some wet wool (vv. 36-40). The wet wool experiment had to be run twice, if you remember, in order for Judge Gideon to be sure. There is nothing wrong with erring on the safe side, but when you are dealing with God there is supposed to be some trust involved. A distant, but somewhat related incident happened in Athens where Paul found a monument or altar labeled "to an unknown god" (Acts 17:22-24). It seems the Athenians had altars to various gods and to be on the safe side, and so as not to leave any god out, they erected an altar to any god they might have missed.

    a. Covering the bases. Where did the phrase, "covering all the bases," originate? Did it mean in baseball having an infielder near each base in case it became the focal point of some action? Did it mean covering all the bases with a tarp when it rains? Did it mean having a runner on each base? Yet, we probably know very well what it means as a cliché: Cover all the possibilities to play it safe, or when in doubt, do the safe thing. There are other ways of wording this sage advice: Plug all the holes, leave no stone unturned, or throw spilled salt over the shoulder just in case there is something to the superstition. It is a good idea to have a "Get out of jail free" card (as in the game Monopoly for those not in the know) in case an occasion for its need should arise. It all sounds like good sound advice. After all, isn't that the principle behind insurance? But what does it look like when applied to religion?

    b. Buying religious insurance. Gideon may have gone overboard testing God. And the Athenians ploy, while cautious, seems a shallow and hollow tribute destined to insult the unknown god. Do some Christians believe in God just in case there is one, but are not sure? In the first church I served, one of our members, who claimed to be an atheist, insisted that his whole family — wife, daughters, and sons — go to church because it would do them good even if there wasn't any God. He was a "good church worker" and a strong church supporter, but he hadn't found God. Some people go to church just to be safe. Some try to do the right thing morally to reserve a seat on the trip to heaven, just in case there is a heaven. It even gets more complicated. We may be careful not to wish any bad to another person, even if we don't like that person, because it may come back on us in some way. A little superstition sends us looking for religious insurance.

c. What's our motive? Should we be on our best behavior because "Candid Camera" or God may be watching, or because we are a person of integrity? Do we act so as not to get caught or punished, or because we are a very moral person? Do we love God and other people and give them our respect just to be safe and because it is the smart thing to do? Is our conduct expedient or compassionate? God is listening, so be careful how you answer that!

T.

T-1. Rainbow-colored Coats And Green-eyed Monsters

Purpose Statement: *I think one of the "seven deadly sins" is jealousy, which may be a temptation for many of us.*

Jacob loved his son Joseph more than all his other sons and showed his preference by making him a beautiful coat or robe (Genesis 37). The coat became a symbol of his brothers' jealousy, causing them to sell him as a slave. It may be difficult to estimate how great a problem jealousy is in our society, however it may be extensive enough to warrant better understanding of the phenomenon and what we can do about it.

    a. Admiration. The more mature we are, the more we are able to admire someone else's good qualities or be happy for their good fortune without being envious. We won't feel threatened by their achievements, nor will we feel a need to measure our success, status, or character by their position. Jealousy occurs when we make what we believe to be unfavorable comparisons between ourselves and others around us. We should admire the gifts of others.

    b. Appreciation. Related to admiration, we should be genuinely pleased about the talents and abilities of others. We should join in the respect and appreciation they receive from others. This is true generosity. We might wonder what the true unexpressed feelings are, of golfers in a tournament, for example. When Hale Irwin is about to make a putt that will tie him with Tom Watson for first place and force a play off, does Watson secretly pray Hale will miss? If Hale makes the putt, is Watson pleased for him? Would it be Christian for one of us in the same circumstance to pray for our opponent to miss, or be resentful if she or he makes the putt?

    c. Justice. Could we at times try to rationalize our jealousy (even give it a different label) by appealing to a sense of justice? We may want to believe another person is in no way deserving of success, being rewarded, winning, or enjoying the respect of others. We consider it a miscarriage of justice. "If others only knew the facts or had any common sense, they would realize the person didn't deserve any accolades or recognition. It isn't fair for someone to get something they don't deserve; and it isn't jealousy on our part, it is simply a keen sense of justice." We know how to cover our petty falls from grace.

d. Selfishness. A good case of the jealousy is grounded on selfishness and greed. We simply "covet our neighbor's house, spouse, cattle," or anything else (Deuteronomy 5:21) he or she might have. Living in a land flowing with milk and honey hasn't been good for our acquisitiveness. "Keep up with the Joneses" may be more than a cute phrase. Possessions may get too much control over us.

e. Envy. One of the main emphases in the dictionary definition for envy stresses hate, anger, ill will, malice, and resentment, among other negatives. This could be much different from a selfish jealousy that focuses on wanting what others have. Envious jealousy focuses on despising the other person. Selfish jealousy may say, "I wish I had her car and she had a better one." Envying jealousy will say, "I want my car and his car and he shouldn't have any." Envy may result from feelings of low self-esteem.

f. Desire. Is a little bit of desire permissible? Is it wrong to have desires for things or qualities other persons might have? It depends. Those desires shouldn't cause you to sell your brother or sister into slavery. Desire should allow us to be pleased for the good fortune of others, and it shouldn't be devastating not to get what we want. It certainly is appropriate to desire God's love and approval, and many other good things in life.

T-2. A Buddhist, A Mormon, And An Atheist Were Out In A Boat Fishing

Purpose Statement: *Dialogue with other faiths and denominations leading to better understanding and cooperation should be an important agenda item for Christians, best achieved in a church setting.*

Our Bible presents two different thoughts regarding relationships with people of other beliefs or religions. The Old Testament makes a strong point of maintaining isolation from people of other religions, and even suggests persecuting them. As an extreme example, Deuteronomy 17:1-7 recommends executing someone who worships other gods or the moon and stars. The Old Testament writers were worried about the possibility that persons exposed to pagan, primitive, or simply other religions would be led astray from the true faith of the Israelites. They were asked not to marry or associate with people of other faiths, and often they were instructed to kill them. As in many other situations, the New Testament position on this issue differs from the Old Testament. We are to be tolerant, kind, and loving toward others. Acts 5:33-39 presents a good example of how we should relate to people of other religions. Some Jews wanted to kill Christians who appeared as threats to the true faith (a la the Old Testament religion). A very wise Pharisee, Gamaliel, suggested a more tolerant and sensible alternative. He said the Jews shouldn't harm the Christians (v. 38), but leave them alone. If the new faith were false, it would die on its own. But if it were of God, it would be wrong to oppose it (v. 39). As Christians, we should be establishing good relations with people of other religions, as well as with Christians of other denominations. Things to keep in mind:
    a. Purpose. As it now stands there are significant barriers and much misunderstanding among Muslims, Jews, Christians, and other religions. There is also suspicion and not enough cooperation between Christians of various denominations. There is so much violence, crime, poverty, and injustice in our world, and the church, because of our unwillingness to

cooperate across denominational lines. We lose much of our potential to create communities of peace and justice and alleviate suffering. It is embarrassing and disappointing to realize there are clergy from different Christian churches who cannot meet together even in social fellowship. We must meet and dialogue to learn to trust and love each other.

b. Attitude. When we approach our sisters and brothers of faith, our attitude cannot be suspicious, nor can it be paternalistic. We cannot behave as if we are superior in our doctrine or our morality. Our tolerance should create an atmosphere of openness, trust, and sincere concern. Our goal is not to *convert* others regardless of what the more conservative among us believe concerning having the only true church. We must listen to other Christians and religious folks as we share our views in an open dialogue.

c. Expectation. I believe Christianity represents the most significant revelation of God and God's will we have. I have read the sacred writings of all major religions and find them incomplete when compared to the teachings of Jesus. Nevertheless, I also believe we have a lot to learn from people of other faiths since we are still struggling with the interpretation of our own scriptures, and they have much truth and love to share. There is a very delicate balance to be maintained. On the one hand, we must firmly believe in our own Christian teachings enough to have a strong, meaningful faith. On the other hand, it must not cause us to be narrow-minded or close-minded. While being very secure in our own faith, we can be open to new thoughts. Finding such a delicate balance is necessary before personal growth will occur.

d. Preparation. Before conversation with others, it is important that we are secure in our own faith. Are we clear or confused? We will find ourselves embarrassed and floundering if we haven't a significant faith. Similar to Gamaliel's advice, if we are secure in our faith, we don't have to worry about being led astray. Our faith should provide

answers to any serious challenges, or else its weaknesses need to be exposed.
   e. Warning. We may be willing to dialogue, and still find serious resistance and unwillingness from other Christians or those from other faiths. There are some religious groups with the conviction that they are right (and the only ones who are) and others are wrong. In these cases there will be no helpful conversations; we just continue to be loving and cooperative whenever, and with whomever, we can.

T-3. A Blueprint For Dying

Purpose Statement: *A Christian should prepare for death and find ways of serving even after death.*

We can understand why some people feel uncomfortable talking about dying or may be unwilling to make any plans for that eventuality. As gruesome as some of us consider the topic, it is one of our Christian responsibilities to make arrangements for our demise and the disbursement of our estates. Jesus wanted to speak about his impending death and Peter rebuked Jesus saying he didn't want to hear of it (Matthew 16:21-23). A few days later Jesus again broaches the subject and disturbs his disciples (Matthew 17:22-23). Jesus tells the parable of the man who was either going to take everything with him when he went or he wasn't going to go (Luke 12:13-20). Jesus ends the story by saying the man could die suddenly and then whose property would all his possessions become? Our responsibility as Christians does not end with death. There are some things we can do from beyond the grave.
   a. Have our funeral decisions made. Because we love our family and friends we can try to bring some convenience and comfort to the grieving process by making arrangements ahead of time. We can make it clear, if it is our intention to reduce the extreme cost of a funeral and burial, so that the family will not be in consternation over difficult decisions. Whatever our wishes, the expediency of letting the family know is an act of thoughtfulness.

b. Plan for responsible disposition of our estates. Christians talk about how God wants us to be good stewards. When we are gone, our stewardship can continue by some deliberate planning that may include church and charity. Seriously, this sermon is not about getting more money for the church. It is solely about our making the most helpful and efficacious distribution of our resources. It is no different than when we are still living. Where does the estate go and what will be the most helpful and considerate? If family and friends are well off, there may be an orphanage, university, soup kitchen, scholarship fund, church, or other charity that could benefit from our gifts.
c. Be an organ or body donor. We have an opportunity of perhaps actually saving a life when we are in our graves. The wonderful act of being an organ donor is becoming a more popular choice as medical science advances in its capacity to repair our bodies. There are individuals living now only because someone who died donated some part of their body as an act of love. Before we get to our graves or are cremated, we have the opportunity to advance life saving medical science by leaving our bodies to a medical school for education. If such a thought sounds frightening or unpalatable to some people, it shouldn't be any more traumatic than knowing our bodies will decay and return to their original elements no matter what route we choose. One of our missions is to care for and serve others.
d. Die with dignity. I visited a young Christian woman dying in the hospital one day. She had a loving husband and three or four young children. She was well aware of the terminal nature of her situation and that death was not far off. She was understandably sad, but nevertheless was able to witness to such courage and love as one rarely sees under such circumstances. I did not minister to her, but instead left the hospital room having been ministered unto.
   1. Our faith and hope should prepare us as Christians to meet death with courage and dignity. Our attitude concerning death can be an inspiration to others.

2. We should decide not to prolong our suffering and waste medical resources beyond any imaginable hope of our recovery.
3. We should help our loved ones by preparing a "living will."

As Christians with the prospects of eternal life awaiting us, we can enter into planning our deaths with a positive attitude, making a statement with our responsible stewardship.

T-4. Developing Extra-Ray Vision

Purpose Statement: *A Christian should become continually more sensitive to his or her total environment.*

One of the first hymns I learned to sing when I started Sunday school at age four was, "Open My Eyes, That I May See." Think about how we get excited over a new wall hanging in our home. It could be an anniversary picture, a beautiful painting, an award we won, or a shadow box of favorite things. We stand back and admire it, perhaps having anticipated the event for some time. Within a week, it has been forgotten and we become so accustomed to its presence that from then on we seldom ever notice it. That may be an analogy of our life's experiences. The other day I read about a 51-year-old man who had surgery on his eyes and was now able to see for the first time in his life. How long do you think it will be before he takes things for granted and fails to fully appreciate his eyesight and the beautiful things around him, as the rest of us do at times? Perhaps in his case, he never will lose his appreciation. However, for most of us, we are missing much enjoyment in life as well as opportunities to serve and make a difference because we are oblivious to much of what is going on around us. As much as I dislike worn-out comments such as, "Are you keeping busy?" there are some that carry poignant suggestions such as, "Stop and smell the roses." Another is, "We can't see the forest for the trees." Jesus on occasion would say, "Let him or her who has ears use them and listen" (Matthew 11:15). I'm sure he said the same thing regarding our eyes and intended to remind us to be observant, alert, aware, knowledgeable, and sensitive. Note how sensitive and alert Jesus was. When a woman in a crowd touched his robe he was aware of it (Luke 8:42a-48) to the amazement of Peter who commented on how people were bumping against him on every side. This sermon could be titled, "Donning Jesus-Colored Spectacles." To be like Jesus we should become more able to ...

    a. Recognize the good in others. Jesus selected questionable people to be his followers: Peter with his flaws, Matthew the tax collector, Judas, Mary Magdalene, and others. He befriended Zacchaeus, another tax collector, and Nicodemus, one of the hostile Pharisees. The people whose lives Jesus salvaged we might relegate to the "lost" column because we consider them evil, unlikable, or hopeless. We may believe there is a spark of the divine, the presence of God, in all persons, since we are all children of God. When we acknowledge this gift and respond appropriately, we can be the kind of loving person that encourages the growth of God's love in others.

    b. Sense when others have needs. The classic moment noted above when the woman touched the edge of Jesus' cloak is indicative of the astuteness we can develop for discerning the problems of those around us. Often when we encounter a grouchy or sullen person and write them off as rude or thoughtless, we need to remember that they may be working through some serious personal problems and need our love and understanding. How many times have we missed an opportunity to minister to the serious needs of those around us? Someone may seem unpleasant and we say, "The heck with you," when a friendly smile and courteous inquiry may be the very thing that changes their lives. If I could do my ministry over, as a pastor I would take the church on field trips to shelters, soup kitchens, and the city mission to help sensitize our selves to the needs of others and the ministry that is happening in the name of Jesus.

c. Detect sin and wrongdoing. Another incident in the life of Jesus, when he revealed his astounding perception, happened when he met with the woman at the well (John 4:5-18). It would be leaping to unwarranted conclusions to pass judgment on the woman and assume Jesus was identifying sin in her life. However, he may have identified some of her concerns, possible problems, and wrong choices she may have made which could account for the broken(?) relationships in her life. Jesus was conscious of the sin in Judas, the weakness in Peter, and the deception in the Pharisees, to enumerate but a few examples. Christians should develop an intuition concerning trouble or potential evil. Through study and diligent observation, we can increase our "street smarts," or our understanding of the reasons why something is wrong or inappropriate for us as Christians.

d. Appreciate the beauty around us. We miss enjoyment because of our visual unawareness, and enjoyment is one of God's gifts to us. We should remind ourselves continually about the miracle of sight and how we are seeing our world in marvelous beautiful color. We have great art, music, and literature to exhilarate us in place of some of the inane television, videos, and movies we waste our time on. So much of how good or bad our experiences will be is determined by the way we make up our minds to interpret or respond to what is going on around us continually. To experience ecstasy, or at least enjoyment, when we behold a beautiful gold and white iris or great fluffy white clouds in an amazing blue sky is evidence of a heightened consciousness and significant sensitivity rewarding us with a fulfilling life. Let her or him who has eyes, see.

Other scriptures might include Isaiah 42:5-7a and 1 Corinthians 13:12.

T-5. Paul Said The Darnedest Things

Purpose Statement: *We cannot ignore some of the strange things Paul said, and we should discuss why he may have said them or why he should not have said them.*

Paul is so important in the history of the church. He probably wrote the first New Testament literature except for some possible memoirs or fragments that may have been used as beginnings for the gospels. As far as we know, Paul was unrivaled in his courageous missionary activity, founding, and working with many early churches. He was very astute in understanding and interpreting Jesus on many issues. For example, his teaching on pacifism is such a close parallel to the teachings of Jesus (Romans 12:9-21 and Matthew 5:38-48). So, why would anyone say Paul said some things that are questionable?

a. Problem. Paul seems to suggest theology and behavior many of us don't accept as appropriate today. How do we deal with these issues? We can illustrate with examples using only the book of 1 Corinthians, some of which have been very divisive for the church.
   1. Paul said (5:9-11) not to associate with sinners, which seems to run contrary to the example Jesus gave us. Aren't we all sinners? This teaching of Paul's has led to lawsuits in the church where persons to be "shunned" were identified, together with their sins, by the pastor from the pulpit.
   2. Paul says it is better not to marry (7:1), remaining single is the preferred state.
   3. If we cannot control ourselves, however, we may marry (7:2). Sounds like a sound reason for marriage?
   4. Women should cover their heads in church, and should not wear their hair cut short (11:5-6).
   5. It is hard not to get the message that Paul was saying men are superior to women (11:7-10), a not too uncommon problem for other religions, as well.
   6. Men should not wear long hair (11:14).

7. Paul suggests the frightening possibility that participating in the Lord's Supper in an unworthy manner could result in our becoming ill or even dying (11:29-30).
8. Paul thinks we should all speak in tongues (14:5).
9. Women should not be church leaders or even speak in church (14:34-35). Consequently, many groups prohibit women from the ranks of the clergy.

b. Options. There are several ways in which we might respond to these teachings including the following six alternatives.
   1. We can try to follow them to the letter. Some fundamentalists do.
   2. We can ignore them and pretend they don't exist. This tends to be the popular choice for many of us.
   3. We can simply say Paul was wrong, but this suggests the Bible has errors in it and makes us very uncomfortable.
   4. We can say it was God's will in Paul's day, but the will of God for today is different. This opens the door to a similar interpretation for all scripture, including the teachings of Jesus.
   5. We could say Paul was speaking only about cultural customs of his day and not stating this was God's will. However, Paul seems to make it sound as if it is God's Law. If it wasn't God's Law, how binding for us should Paul's suggested cultural practices be?
   6. We could confess that we don't understand any of it and remain confused. Are there other possibilities?

c. Solution. First, we should be prepared to continue our struggle with all the teachings of Paul as well as in all other scriptures. We have plenty of room to grow. Personally, I would choose a combination of options 3 and 5 in the list above. Paul (option 5) was definitely influenced by the mores and customs of his day, and we do need to obey some cultural rules (today's) to have an orderly society.

However, in some instances, it is necessary to make significant changes in the current ways of doing things. Finally, as uncomfortable as it will be, we may have to say Paul was wrong (option 3) regarding some of his conjectures concerning the teachings of Jesus or the will of God. Our ultimate decision as to what to accept and what to reject in the teachings of Paul rests in the teachings of Jesus. Everything Paul taught must be analyzed using the comprehensive life and teachings of Jesus. When there is a consensus in the teaching of the two men, Paul is right. However, when what Paul says goes against the nature and spirit of Christ (for example, the value and role of women, improper communion could kill you), we should follow Jesus and ignore Paul. In the last analysis, we are Christians and Jesus is the unequaled revelation of God for us.

T-6. Does The Sneaky Side Of Us Enjoy Violence?

Purpose Statement: *How unhealthy is the obsession we have with violence and what can the Christian do about it?*

Why is our country one of the most violent in the world? This is a major concern for all of us; however, we don't seem to take enough serious action to make a difference. Most of us fantasize concerning a world of peace and justice. The ideal could be the "peaceful kingdom" described in Isaiah 65:17-25. It would be full of joy; there would be no crying or suffering, no disaster. Babies will not die in infancy; wolves and lions will not harm lambs and cows. We know we cannot have a perfect society, but we can do so much better than we are currently doing to make our world safe and happy. Jesus listed some secrets for individual happiness. Be humble, merciful, pure in heart, sensitive, and peace-makers (Matthew 5:3-10). He said when we take up the sword; we will die by the sword (Matthew 26:52) — something we haven't begun to understand yet. Jesus comments that the world mistakenly believes violence to be a viable solution to many problems, but his kingdom is different and people do not fight or kill (John 18:36). Violence is so pervasive in our nation.

    a. Where it is now. More of our citizens (per capita) are in prison than almost any other country in the world. Isn't this a terrible indictment? Isn't anyone amazed and concerned? We have more gun deaths (per capita) than any other industrialized country. Young people take guns to school and kill their classmates and teachers. Employees are gunning down their co-workers. Serial killers and snipers draw our attention because of the media hype, but they represent a small portion of the murders committed regularly in our country. (Eighty percent of the guns possessed by criminals have been stolen from legitimate gun owners making them and the NRA responsible for most of the guns used in criminal activity.) Survivalists stockpile weapons to use against their neighbors and their government. Newspapers carry many stories of fights in nightclubs and bars that result in injuries and deaths. Violence is prevalent in our sports world and includes spectators. Recently, Ohio State won a national championship and the fans burned cars and looted as part of the celebration. These were the winners — not the losers. Finally, violence with our automobiles is unbelievable.

    b. Where it is coming from. There are numerous origins. It begins with our country's lingering frontier mentality. It also involves poor parenting skills; people who can't manage their own lives keep having children. Violence in our media must accept its share of blame. Movies with excessive violence — car bombings and crashes, shootings, and other destruction — are extremely popular and influential. Guns have proliferated into everyone's hands. Hunting statistics indicate there are many people who enjoy killing animals. Video games are violent; some modern music videos spew out sick lyrics and violent gyrations; war is constant in our world; boxing and wrestling (despite the latter's being fake) are popular. While we criticize bull fighting in other countries, dog and cock fighting are still legal in some states and even exist where they are illegal. It is hard to believe there are still people today who will say these things have no effect on our society. Studies have shown strong correlations between watching violence and becoming desensitized to violence, and even becoming violent. It seems as if only a small percent of our population is offended by war, or shocked by the carnage. We have a morbid curiosity of serial killers and disasters.

c. Where it is going. The portrayal of violence in our media and entertainment leads to a desensitization as well as proneness to violence in our own lives. Violence begets violence. We are concerned over abuse to spouses and children that is increasing in our society, but our solutions are more like first-aid after the fact, such as "safe houses" and counselors (both of which are very important) rather than prevention. It would seem obvious one solution is to not allow our children (and ourselves) to watch such destruction. Unsurprisingly, if a church posts a ban on certain movies, television programs, or books, the effect is to increase the prohibited viewing or reading. Christians are not a lot different than non-Christians in this regard. We should encourage workshops and studies on the matter, followed by social action: visiting legislators, protesting, and letter writing. People are being hurt; not enough is being done. Jesus weeps over the city once again.

T-7. When Religion Turns Into A Circus

Purpose Statement: *Why does religion sometimes become bizarre, weird, or ridiculous, and what do we do about it?*

As improbable as it seems, the early Christian church at Corinth had allowed its services, and particularly its communion services, to become corrupted. In his letter, Paul (1 Corinthians 11:17-22) scolded the members over the way they conducted themselves at communion. There were people present who didn't understand what the church was about and they became a disrupting influence. Knowing the reasons why religion could turn into a circus should help us know how to stay within the parameters of good, sound faith and intelligent behavior in our church life.

    a. The circus comes to town. Some people find amusement in the bizarre behavior of some church groups, cults, or eccentric religious individuals. Other people consider them pathetic. All of us should be concerned. History has provided dramatic examples of embarrassing activities in the name of Christian religion. August 1801, 25,000 Christians gathered at Cane Ridge, Kentucky, for a religious camp meeting. After being possessed by the spirit some found their bodies jerking and contorting, while others gathered around trees and barked like dogs in order to tree the devil. Copious use of a different kind of *spirits* may have enhanced the performance. We don't have to look very far back in history to find a group of Christians holding hands and marching around the casket of a dead boy (who died because his faith prohibited medical care) as they prayed expecting God to raise him from the dead. Such "far out" displays are more rare and thus, perhaps, less disturbing than more common practices or beliefs that are less bizarre but still stray beyond good sense. Some of our Christian religious behavior and doctrine may approach the outlandish, ridiculous, or even harmful. In general, there are wings or sects of the Christian church that can be more bizarre and embarrassing at times than almost any other institution or organization.

    b. Send in the clowns. We inappropriately label folks with very strange or wild religious beliefs or behavior as "nuts" or "weirdos." We wonder why religion would attract people prone to strange ideas and behavior. There are some very good reasons.

        1. Religion is very personal and speaks to our deepest and most personal needs. It encompasses the entire spectrum of our lives.

2. People with serious problems expect to find acceptance in the church or Christian faith. Christians will love and care for the needy, which naturally attracts disturbed and confused persons.
3. Religion has a mystery about it. God is a mystery; death and eternal life are veiled; so much of it has a supernatural tone.
4. Religion is connected with miracles and this creates expectations of the impossible or highly improbable.
5. The Bible itself doesn't help matters with certain passages giving cryptic comments such as "the life is in the blood" (Leviticus 17:14) leading some to refuse blood transfusions.

The Bible suggests women should not speak in church (1 Corinthians 14:33-34), we can drink poison with impunity (Mark 16:18), stars will fall from the skies (Matthew 24:29), the moon will turn red as blood (Acts 2:20), and we could be moved to babble in tongues. These are examples of the many other enigmatic passages in our Bible. It is not difficult to see how our religion could have an unhealthy appeal for the persons with mental or personality problems.

c. Be a lion tamer. We must support, encourage, and practice a wholesome Christian faith. What we believe and practice must be intellectually respectable; it must be logical, sensible, and realistic. It must be capable of building healthy relationships, creating supportive communities, and providing environments of trust and understanding. We must never shun the lonely, needy, or "strange." A Christian endeavors to supply whatever resources people with problems need. The more our churches provide wholesome environments for good mental health, the fewer bizarre religious practices we will see.

T-8. You *Can* Learn To Like Spinach, Liver, And Theology

Purpose Statement: *We need to overcome our resistance to Sunday school and Bible study.*

We are making a big assumption that most people have an aversion to study which would include going to Sunday school, doing Bible study, and discussing religion and theology. For those who like it and do it, bless you. For those who don't like it, the following important message is for you. Remember when God told Eve and Adam in the Garden of Eden not to eat of the tree of knowledge (Genesis 2:15-17)? After all these years it finally dawned on me that that was a trick God pulled on the woman and man to actually get them to eat the forbidden fruit. It always bothered me why God would not want us to have knowledge, but now I see that God knew if the woman and man were told not to study and learn, that is just what they would do, just as the first thing we do when we see a "Wet Paint — do not touch" sign, is touch it. Did God use reverse psychology on them? Now that I have let the cat out of the bag, I suppose it is too late to use that same reverse psychology on you, and urge you not to taste of the tree of knowledge. The truth is that God wants us to grow in knowledge and understanding. Just as Jesus was eager to discuss theology with the religious leaders in the temple even when he was a young boy (Luke 2:41-50), we also can develop a passion for Bible study and Sunday school.

    a. Why we resist theology. What is it about educational activities that causes us to dislike them? Could it be we consider it work? Do we think we don't have the time? Is it because we believe Sunday school and Bible study are boring? Do we consider the subject matter boring or not relevant to our needs? We must discover how important it is and how satisfying it can become.

    b. Why we should learn to like theology. Theology is at the heart of life. It is concerned about all of God's world, what it is like, how we should relate to our total environment, as well as the secrets of building meaningful relationships with others. Theology should be the basic foundation of our knowledge and our behavior. It should be the center of our philosophy of life, the origin of our principles, and the focus for all our goal setting. We may find ourselves in one of two categories.

1. Some folks believe they are proficient in religion and psychology (and they probably aren't). They erroneously believe they have a healthy foundation of beliefs and a good common sense. Apparently not enough of us are really as mature as we think or we wouldn't have a world with so much conflict, poverty, violence, anger, crime, and domestic abuse. We may not appreciate what we are missing until we seriously explore our faith and theology.
2. The rest of us acknowledge our theological deficiency and believe it is all too complicated for our limited capacity.

c. How to learn to like theology. When I was a senior in college I saw two roommates playing chess. I didn't know how the game was played, and since I despised checkers, I knew I would also dislike chess as well. Yet, I wanted to know what it was all about because it was a popular game and part of our culture, even though I was convinced I would never like the game. I at least wanted to be knowledgeable even if I never played the game again. I asked my roommates to teach me all about chess and I immediately became excited about the game. It has provided me with much enjoyment over the years. There was once a product advertised with the slogan, "Try it; you'll like it." We need to expose ourselves to theology: discuss the nature of God and what it means to be a Christian. If it doesn't take with one bite, try a few more bites. Patience and persistence should bring very satisfying rewards. When we become thoroughly immersed in theology, we will find it not just interesting, but possibly fascinating, enjoyable, and certainly very helpful. If someone, after sufficient attempts, still is unable to become excited over theology, that rare individual should grit her or his teeth and do Bible study and Sunday school anyway. We probably don't enjoy a visit to the dentist, but it is a wise thing to do. While it will take some individuals more effort than others, everyone can grow to appreciate and even enjoy discussions concerning God's will and what it means to be a Christian.

T-9. A Bodyguard Named Jesus

Purpose Statement: *It is certainly appropriate and important to ask ourselves what our motive is, or our reason for becoming a follower of Jesus.*

Why are you a Christian? Usually we have reasons for the things we do even though they may not be clearly understood, because we may not have thought them through carefully. Unknown to us, unconscious or hidden motives could exist that haven't surfaced yet. Why we became a Christian is something we may have taken for granted, and the reason might surprise us. Under most circumstances we ask, "What's in it for me?" Are the reasons we became a Christian altruistic or selfish? (This, then, translates into what our appeal to others to accept Jesus will be.) Some promotion schemes assure us we can make fortunes by using their secret: for example, a plan to buy land with no down payment and sell it for big profits. Another company wants us to sell their superior products under a pyramid arrangement where we may become wealthy by enlisting others to sell for us. The "come on" is a thinly veiled pitch that we would be providing a good product, while the real catch is an appeal to greed and how it will bring us great wealth. Returning to our faith, we must ask, "Why are we Christians, and what message are we using to attract others?"

    a. Protection from misfortune. Even many of our hymns are couched in the promise that God will take care of us. Have some individuals "committed their lives to Christ" with the hope that the benefits will include being spared misfortune? Even though most of us know better, we still cling to the superstition that good things attend good people and bad things happen to bad people. Instead of Christianity sheltering us from misfortunes, actually, Jesus warned his followers that being a disciple entailed suffering and persecution (Luke 21:12; Matthew 5:10-11; 8:19-20).

b. Get to heaven. It would be a shame if the sole reason for becoming a Christian was to insure our going to heaven. Such an arrangement sounds like bribery. It would be as bad as knowing the only reason we don't rob and steal was because we were afraid of being caught and punished. Having integrity and character means we can be trusted, are not selfish, and we do things because we love and care for others instead of what might be in it for us. Matthew 19:16-22 records an incident where a rich man came to Jesus looking for the secret of eternal life. He wasn't really interested much in the suggestion Jesus made concerning helping others, so he went away preferring possessions instead of salvation. Jesus tells us that being a disciple isn't really about getting into heaven.

c. Get "in good" with God. We want our teachers, employers, friends, and others to like us and think well of us. Some of our behavior results from needing their approval. There should be no one we would desire to please more than God. By following Jesus, it makes God pleased with us. Careful scrutiny is necessary to determine if our desire to please God is because we love God and others, and we live honest, loving lives to honor God, our family, and friends out of respect, or not.

d. Feel good about ourselves. Even at our best there may be a little sneaky selfishness lurking around. Can we ever be purely altruistic? Perhaps some personal satisfaction isn't all that bad. Good deeds bring an appropriate satisfaction that isn't wrong as long as it doesn't constitute our entire motive.

e. Because we know it is the right thing to do. This, and the desire to help others out of love, are perfect reasons for becoming followers of Jesus. We accept Christ and do good, not because Jesus will become our heavenly bodyguard, but for the simple reason we know it is what we should do, and because we love God and others.

T-10. From Inside A Really Big Empty

Purpose Statement: *Because many of us do not recognize our need for God, we find substitutes (sometimes dangerous ones) to fill the vacuum.*

Ever want something but you aren't sure what it is? Something is missing and we can't put our finger on it. There is a restlessness we can't explain. Psalm 42 has the answer: "As a deer longs for water, our soul thirsts for God" (vv. 1-2). When our spirits are depressed or we experience emptiness within, our hope and help is in God (vv. 5 and 11). While generally viewed as pessimistic, the book of Ecclesiastes is about this void caused by a missing God. The writer spends considerable time explaining how we seek for meaning in all kinds of things only to find all of them unsatisfying. The first chapter begins with a vivid description of the uselessness and unfulfilling nature of so much of life. Finally, at the end of the book (12:13) we read that there is only one answer: We were created for God.

    a. Vacuums must be filled. There are voids in our lives to be filled that we identify as "needs." We need food, purpose, love, companionship, rest, renewal, recreation, goals, and most of all, God. God has created us for relationship. As the great commandment reminds us, we must "love God with all we have and love our neighbor as our self." Physics teaches, "Nature abhors a vacuum." Just as water pours through a hole in the bottom of a boat, whatever is present and possible will rush into an empty space to fill it. This physical law of the universe is paralleled in the spiritual realm. Something will always fill the emptiness:
    1. If not love, then hate or indifference.
    2. If not righteousness, then evil or greed.

3. If not God, then possessions. We cannot serve two masters ... (Matthew 6:24).
 b. We don't know what we are missing. Occasionally someone says, "I don't feel complete." An article told of a young woman who didn't feel "balanced" until she had a large tattoo engraved across most of her back. It probably wasn't long before she felt unbalanced once more and began looking for another false hope. Because we don't always recognize our real needs, we search in strange places. Substitutes, to fill the void created when God is missing include: work (perhaps becoming a workaholic), hobbies, sex, food (overeating), wealth, alcohol and other drugs, some of the many recreational activities (partying, skiing, driving around, video games, and such), and even strange religions.
 c. Accept no substitutes. Just because we fill the void doesn't mean we are satisfied. If our stomachs are empty and we fill them with water only, it will not suffice. Sooner or later we must satisfy that emptiness with what is really needed. Jesus tells the parable of the man who thought he would have it all if he just built bigger barns for his crops (Luke 12:16-21). Jesus concluded that he was "not rich in God's sight." Jesus continues by saying clothes, food, nor anything else will be able to satisfy us without God (vv. 22-30). The secret, he said, was to seek first God's kingdom and everything else will find its proper meaning (v. 31). We need
    1. the awareness of God's presence for ultimate fulfillment,
    2. a faith that answers our needs and questions, and
    3. activities that serve others in the name of God.

U.

U-1. Watch Those Promises!

Purpose Statement: *Christians need to be careful concerning making promises, and then know how to deal with the guilt of broken promises.*

Judges 11:30-40 records a terrible story that hopefully is apocryphal. We would like to believe this didn't really happen. Jephthah is leading the Israelites in battle against the Ammonites and promises God that if he is given the victory he will burn as an offering the first person he meets coming out of his house when he returns home. Of course, the first person to greet him on his return is his daughter who runs out excited and happy to see her daddy. Jephthah believes his promise to God is sacred and offers his daughter as a sacrifice. Where was the ram caught in the bush (Genesis 22:13)?

    a. God doesn't make deals. It would be mistaken to believe that we can bargain with God. We can't offer to do something *if* God will reward us in some way in return. Yet sometimes our superstition causes us to believe by accepting some task for God, doing some good deed or by mending our ways, God will give us some benefit. "God, I will stop cursing if you give our team the victory in this tournament." "God, I will go to church every Sunday unless its raining, if you will help me get this job." We will even fool ourselves into believing what we want is so important and so right that God must want it, also, enhancing the probability that God will be willing to deal with us. Unfortunately, Jephthah was mistaken in believing that God gave him the victory over the Ammonites and that God desired the daughter as a burnt offering.

    b. Be careful what you promise. Jephthah had to be out of his mind to make such a promise. Ecclesiastes 5:1-7 cautions us to think carefully about our commitments before we make them (v. 2). It is important to keep promises (v. 4), it reflects on our trustworthiness and integrity, and we should treat promises made to others as promises made to God. Our wedding vows are usually done in a worship setting and a Christian service, and should be considered promises to God as well as to our partner. If promises made to others are not kept, it reflects on our faith. Ecclesiastes admonishes us not to make any commitments at all rather than make them and break them (v. 5). It may be appropriate here to discuss what Jesus meant (Matthew 5:33-37) by his comments on vows. His words were tantamount to saying to "swear on the Bible" is superfluous or totally unnecessary. As a Christian our *word* is entirely trustworthy. We only need to say "Yes" or "No" and that is sufficient. To have to certify our word with, "Cross my heart and hope to die, stick a needle ..." is to suggest that without such substantiation we cannot be trusted.

c. Don't keep bad promises. Let's take a vote; how many think Jephthah was wrong to keep his promise? It seems to be unanimous. The sin against his daughter was many times worse than a broken agreement, even one made to God. We must always weigh the difference between the lesser of two evils. Keeping a rash or foolish commitment that will result in further harm or an unfortunate act is compounding the mistake.

d. How do we resolve guilt over broken promises? Our character is at stake. If we cannot keep our word, it is a blight on our integrity. However, as just mentioned, it is entirely inappropriate to keep a harmful contract. The guilt should be over making an inappropriate pact in the first place, and not in breaking it. Breaking it was part of the remedy in a bad situation. On the other hand, we must repent and seek forgiveness when we fail to keep pledges that merit our solemn word. If the promise was worthy, we must deal with the guilt of breaking it as we would other sins. Reparations to the injured party may be called for to right wrongs and salvage our character as Christians.

U-2. Is The Bible Racist?

Purpose Statement: *Can we find any racism in our Bible?*

Haven't we all heard the statement that whatever the issue, we will be able to find passages in scripture to support both sides of the position? Biblical passages will be cited to support the use, as well as the abolition of capital punishment; the permission to use, as well as the prohibition of alcoholic beverages; the support and also the condemnation of war, the permission and denial for divorce: that homosexuality is and is not a sin, and so forth. What about racism? The Bible has been quoted to justify slavery and segregation in the past, even though we all know both are contrary to God's will. Can we see vestiges of racist attitudes in scripture today? No! You will find verses recommending burnt offerings, stoning, and other unfortunate practices, but nothing of a racist nature. Let us consider four thoughts.

    a. Slavery. There are certainly passages in our Bible that seem to support slavery, *but not by race.* Exodus 21 clearly indicates that slavery was not associated with race or ethnicity. Jews were enslaved by fellow Jews. People of all races owned slaves of all races. There was no race distinction associated with slavery. Christians have made a case for slavery using Paul's letter to Philemon. But the race of neither Philemon nor Onesimus is known, and is not an issue.

    b. Segregation. Again, there is no doubt that segregation is recommended in parts of our Bible, but in every case it *is not associated with race.* Segregation pertained to differences of religions. The people, particularly in Old Testament periods, believed God did not want the Israelites living with, or marrying, people of other religions. The fear was Israelites would stray from the true worship and religion. Race was totally unrelated. Examples would include Exodus 23:27-33 and 34:10-16.

    c. Passages cited for racism. It would be impossible to consider every passage someone might conjure up to support racism, however, the favorite ones usually quoted are easily dismissed as erroneous. One popular source is the curse on Ham pronounced by *Noah, not* by *God* (Genesis 9:18-27), and it was a curse on Semitic peoples (Canaan), not just Africans. The tower of Babylon story is about languages, not races (Genesis 11:1-9). Both Ezra and Nehemiah prohibited mixed marriages, but not according to race, but by and because of differences in religions.

d. Passages cited against racism. John 4:5-27 has Jesus relating to a Samaritan woman (one whom Jews would discriminate against) in an unacceptably familiar way for the culture of his day. Luke 10:25-37 makes the hero or good person a Samaritan. Philemon 1:15-16 urges Onesimus to accept his slave as a "dear brother." Galatians 3:26-29 tells us there is no difference between slaves and free men, races, or gender; we are all one. Ephesians 2:11-18 again reminds us we are all one body, not separate races. Paul rebukes Peter for inappropriate and unacceptable racist behavior (Galatians 2:11-14). The Sermon on the Mount says we are to love all people, even our enemies, and treat them all equally (Matthew 5:43-44, 47). Song of Songs 1:4-6 claims dark skin is beautiful. Abraham, Joseph, Moses, David, Solomon, and others took wives from other nations and races.

This is only a beginning. When preaching this subject, you will find many other supportive biblical references.

U-3. The Four Most Beautiful Things God Ever Created

Purpose Statement: *A Christian should be a person with a highly developed sense of aesthetics.*

Part of my theory of beauty is that when we grow close to God and experience love in our lives, we develop a greater appreciation for beauty. Psalm 8 is a hymn of beauty and praise of God to remind us of our blessings. It describes the four most beautiful things God created.

a. The universe. My imagination is always stretched to the exhausting point when I read about astronomy. Psalm 8, one of the few nature passages in our Bible, draws our attention to God's greatness in the universe of heavens, galaxies, stars, and moons (vv. 1 and 3). So much of our scripture is given to instructions for proper personal behavior, theology, and history, there is so little room left for the praise of God's world of nature. Evidence from modern telescopes suggests a universe with billions of galaxies, and each galaxy as having billions of stars. Distances are beyond our comprehension. Light travels so fast, it could go around the earth seven and a half times in a second, and yet at that speed the light from the nearest star took about four years to get here! The light from most of the stars we see in the night sky started from the star before we were born. The greatness of the universe and thus the greatness of our God is fantastic.
b. The world. It is not our best evidence of eternal life, but the world of nature is so wonderful that when I marvel at the beauty of clouds of infinite variety, mountains, canyons, all kinds of trees, sunsets, waterfalls, rainbows, and the eyes to see it all, I am compelled to say there is too much wonder and joy in our world not to last. How can there be so much beauty and so little time to experience it? For some people the time is very brief. All this staggering variety of beauty says to me, "The world is good and filled with hope." Psalm 8:7-9 mentions the animals, birds, and fish. Visit a zoo, a large aquarium, or a botanical garden and if you are not significantly impressed with the simply amazing variety of creatures and the astounding colors of flowers, salt water fish, and birds, you need a wake up call.
c. Little things. The older we grow, the more we treasure everything about God's creation, even the little things. My wife and I used to think an exciting vacation was a visit to places like Bryce Canyon, Arches National Park, and Glacier Park. Age has given us more wisdom, and

now walking through the neighborhood after the first good snow or on a colorful autumn day is an exciting adventure packed with rich beauty. Not only is all nature prized, but other tangible and intangible gifts. Trinkets that have nostalgic value, good music, food, a cozy bed, a beautiful black and white Holstein cow, a good book, and plays are treasures. We thank God for the intangibles that include love, freedom, peace, humor, fun, opportunities, forgiveness, and innumerable sensations. Psalm 8:6 tells us we have been placed over all creation.

d. You and me. A Christian, more than any other person, should recognize the beauty in other people. This is not the outward appearance that is inappropriately glorified in such things as beauty pageants. I read a great book on this subject the other day titled, *Frankenstein and Miss America: Who's Who and Who's Not.* This is a riveting book that should be "must" reading for everyone. The beauty that mature people appreciate is an inner spirit. Each person has a unique personality of gifts that make her or him interesting and enjoyable. The more mature we become, the greater our sensitivity to such beauty. Psalm 8 tells us we were created only a little less than angels or God (v. 5) and crowned with glory and honor. To be honest, too many of us find it extremely difficult to get past appearances. We are excited by physical attractiveness and repulsed by what we term ugliness. It takes a lot of God's love in us before we grow to cherish each person as special and enjoy the true beauty of his or her special gifts.

When our aesthetics have been sharpened to this level, it causes us to be more concerned with sharing with others and building the kind of just and peaceful world which others can more fully enjoy. While God's love brings about this savoring of our world, in turn such sensitivity causes us to experience even more of God's love.

U-4. Did The Wise Men Sleep In The Stable?

Purpose Statement: *The Christian should be sensitive to, and concerned about, the abuse of privilege.*

That special people get special treatment is a well-known fact. One fine example in our Old Testament concerns Solomon (1 Kings 10:1-5, 10). The Queen of Sheba paid Solomon a visit and felt compelled to bring him lavish gifts: jewels and spices by the camel load, and almost five tons of gold. If the gifts she brought didn't amaze her, the scriptures tell us she was breathless when she saw the splendor that surrounded him. You say why not, after all, he was the king. That's our point. People we consider *special* get preferential treatment, the more celebrated they are the greater the privilege. Consider the Wise Men who visited Jesus at his birth (Matthew 2:1-2, 9-11). If there was *no room in the inn*, where do you suppose they stayed? They came from far off lands and would not have been able to travel back home without staying over. You say by the time they arrived, Jesus' family had found better quarters and accommodations had opened up in the inn, or they traveled on that day to a village down the road where rooms were available. Stop, you are spoiling my story. The point we are considering is that the Wise Men, wealthy and prestigious as they were, probably did not sleep in the stable, as did Mary and Joseph. Suddenly, a room in the inn would have become available. Privilege happens for special people.

    a. Some have it. Privilege is all around us. Special treatment for important people, that is unattainable by the rest of us, is observed when someone with influence gets a table in a restaurant when we have been told the place has no tables available. We have heard of individuals who have friends working at sports events who let them into ball games free. How many times have we heard about traffic tickets being fixed by people knowing the right people? Recently in our community, a police officer was stopped for a traffic violation by another officer, but was not given a citation. We were told that it needed to be *investigated* later. I wonder if I can suggest that arrangement the next time (oops), I mean *if* I ever get stopped?

b. We resent it. If the person receiving preferential treatment is a friend or someone we like, we overlook their indulgence. However, if they are someone we don't know or care about, we will be incensed. Our sense of fair play resents someone receiving benefits denied the rest of us. Someone crowding in line ahead of us does not endear herself or himself to all those in line behind.

c. Unless we get it. Have you ever gotten into a movie or a sports event because you knew the ticket taker or a person at the gate? Be honest now, you felt pretty good about your coup. Part of the fun was being able to tell everyone about it afterward. "I *know* people; I got a special deal." If the friends, whom we tell about our good fortune, are very astute, they will feel the insult. Any special privilege we receive (an exemption, license, tax break, free admission to an event, or other benefits) is given, in fact, at their expense, or is something that has been denied them. When we find a clever or sneaky way of gaining advantage without supporting the cause, someone else will have to shoulder the cost. We might as well laugh in the faces of our friends with a, "Ha, ha, I got a special deal on a new car because I know someone. You, on the other hand, will pay more for your car to make up for what I didn't pay." When the Christian faith is able to maintain special privilege in our country with prayers in legislative sessions or having the Bible read in schools, we are taking advantage of being in the majority and thumbing our noses at the other religious groups. If we are interested in *winning* their cooperation, we are not going about it in the proper fashion. We must examine our feelings about privilege. Is it disturbing when someone else gets it, but a welcome gift when we are the beneficiaries? How would Jesus feel about it? One parable Jesus told illustrates the situation clearly. Matthew 18:23b-34 should be examined carefully.

U-5. When Kids Go Bad

Purpose Statement: *What is the cause of so many of the problems our youth have today and what can the church do about it?*

Far too many of our young people today are having serious difficulties. It ranges from simple family squabbles where parents and youth have poor communication and poor relationships, to the more serious involvement in gangs and drug activity. Christians want to find ways to serve our youth and help them find the kind of enjoyable and trouble-free teen years that they deserve.

    a. There is far more pressure on our youth today than ever before. My teen years were the '50s and there were never the kind of drug problems we are experiencing now. Gangs were few and far between. Kids still got into trouble and young people got pregnant. However, the peer pressure is greater today, and the media has helped to create an environment of increasing permissiveness. Parents complain of lack of communication with their children and teens, and relationships are poor. Why do kids get involved in gangs, do drugs, or harass other kids? There are multiple answers to that question, but we will consider only one cause.

    b. I believe *low self-esteem* and *insecurity* are what's up with youth. Among a variety of reasons, low self-esteem has to stand at the top of the list. Insecurity drives them into gang fellowships where they think they will find acceptance. It is lack of self-respect that encourages drug use and the abuse of other peers. When they don't feel good about themselves they need peer acceptance, which means a strong desire to dress the right way, to be brainwashed into accepting what passes for music today, and the need to form cliques. Jesus considered each child precious (Matthew 18:2-7) and would want them to be a central focus for the church's ministry.

    c. The answer to low self-esteem is love and acceptance. Each of us needs to feel we belong to a team or fellowship where we find we count for something. Some church people will pontificate a simple, vague answer such as, "They need to get right with God, that's all." But it is much deeper than that. To start with, what does that really mean, and could you communicate that meaning to youth? The answer to the problem is making each child and youth feel that they are important to the rest of us. We respect their uniqueness, independence, and character and relate to them as real human beings. It starts at the earliest age. Proverbs 22:6 tells us to teach a young child all about love and meaningful relationships, and they will grow into healthy, wholesome adults. This doesn't mean uninhibited permissiveness, but correction and direction (Proverbs 29:15 and 17). It is possible to be a loving parent and friend, and yet provide loving discipline and guidance, and to nurture young persons into mature and responsible persons. It still happens. When you truly respect them and spend time in significant relationships, they learn respect for others. The church must initiate programs for youth that have quality and value. We must have mature expectations of their talents. Mentoring can be vital for troubled youth, or those with special needs. The church is the one institution offering all a person needs to find a sense of worth and dignity. We offer caring, love, respect, trust, and fellowship. That is the kind of God we serve.

U-6. Methinks Thou Dost Not Protest Too Much

Purpose Statement: *This sermon presents the case for Christians becoming social activists.*

Scripture has its share of social activists. Moses intervened in a slavery issue (Exodus 2:11-13) in Egypt, had to flee the country, and later went back to get re-involved once more as God directed a campaign of protests to free all the slaves. Jeremiah demonstrated against the war with the Babylonians (Jeremiah 11:18-23; 27:1-12) pleading for peaceful submission on the part of Judah instead of armed resistance. The hawks complained to the king accusing Jeremiah of undermining the courage of the soldiers and the war effort (38:1-6). That sounds familiar. Amos (2:6-8) fought, among other things, predatory lenders in his community. History doesn't seem to change much over the years. Amos cried out against the growing gap between the rich and the very poor because of the corruption of his society, which included injustice in the courts (4:1-3; 5:10-15). Jesus gave us an example of a dramatic demonstration in Jerusalem when he ran the vendors and moneychangers from the temple (John 2:13-16). On one occasion, Jesus was told by the Pharisees to silence his disciples. They were saying things that irritated the Pharisees, and Jesus defended them, saying, "If the disciples were to keep silence, the very stones would cry out." In other words, we cannot sit by and let injustices and travesty go unchallenged. Righteousness, peace, and justice must be heard if it takes the stones to speak. Will the church be a dynamic force for social change in the world or will we just *talk* about the love of Jesus in whispers behind our walls and hope someday enough people will decide to be nice?

   a. Get informed. We know the issues since we are bombarded with the painful news every day. Just the war issue itself, among so many other vital concerns, commands our attention. We constantly prepare for war with more money and resources than for any other program, instead of preparing for peace. Since we haven't learned how to prepare for peace and get along internationally as adults, we are always under the threat of military conflict. Our method of violent physical force hasn't worked yet; wars and threat of wars continue on and on. We may not enjoy the task of reading and research on those social issues that are devastating our society, but it is mandated that we diligently study the concerns and become extremely well informed as churches and Christians.

   b. Get organized. We need to get the church involved in these studies (see sermon Z-9, "We Need To Talk") where we can begin to grow in our consensus of what is at stake and just what God desires the church to do. God led the entire

Bible leaders mentioned in the scriptures above. If we were to give prayerful, open minded study to social concerns, we would gravitate toward an understanding of God's will for our church and us as Christians (see sermon F-10, "What Are You Doing Out Of Jail?"). We need to form groups in our churches, as well as groups among neighborhood churches across denominational lines.

c. Get going. There is no excuse for not doing letter writing campaigns, protest marches, and visits to legislators. We must let our leaders know what we feel is right and seek to educate the rest of our communities. The civil rights demonstrations of the '60s taught us a great lesson. Serious social issues that destroy people's lives do not change until someone stands up and says something. The church has a choice of being either a leader or a follower.

U-7. Noah And The Ark And Other True Stories

Purpose Statement: *How do we interpret the improbable sounding stories in our Old Testament?*

Every Christian, except for the fundamentalists, at some time will ask the question, "Are the extravagant stories of our Bible really true?" Did Daniel survive the lions' den? Did a snake talk to Eve? Did a big fish swallow Jonah and spit him back up again? Were there really supernatural beings mating with humans, and giants as their offspring (Genesis 6:1-4)? Did people build a tower in Babylon that was so high it worried God? Is it conceivable that a man named Noah built a boat large enough to save every species of animal from a flood that covered the entire earth? People probably wonder why such stories appear mainly in the Old Testament, or why there haven't been events of that caliber throughout history, or even today. It is not easy to preach this sermon, but integrity calls for the preacher to be forthright with church members. There is no alternative.

a. The options. Very generally, we could say there are two options as to how one interprets these stories. First and most obvious, we can assume the stories are literally true word for word. We could believe the earth was created in six days our time, and each day 24 hours. Very conservative Christians insist on a literal interpretation of scriptures because they fear when the literal truth of one story is questioned, where does one stop? If the story of Noah and the ark is a myth, does that mean Jesus could be a myth? This is a seriously valid enough question not to be lightly brushed aside. The fundamentalists will also worry that such a figurative interpretation may make God out to be a liar somehow. Our second option is to understand the stories as myths, to be interpreted figuratively and symbolically. Instead of being factual history, they could be like the stories Jesus told. When Jesus told a parable, for example, the parable of the sower (Matthew 13:1-9), he did not intend us to think it actually happened. His intention is to tell a story that directs our attention to a moral. When asked why he used parables, Jesus answered in a cryptic way, that apparently only those who were really sincere in their quest for truth or prepared to follow would understand (Matthew 13:10-17). Could it be the very conservative Christian, who insists on the literal understanding, is closing his or her opportunities for understanding the deeper meaning of these stories in the way intended? The Pharisees were celebrated for their literal interpretation of the law.
b. The truth. When we say the Bible is true, our statement is true. The Bible has no intention of misleading or deceiving. Scripture represents an honest and sincere approach to the truth of God and God's will. The figurative interpretation is a much more sophisticated approach to truth, in general. On this level, the story of Noah and the ark is not concerned with history, but is struggling with theological truth. The issue is over sin and evil in the world, and the

need for our renewal or regeneration. A literal interpretation makes God a terribly violent and vindictive God, doing things only the worst of us would do. To defend the idea that God really flooded the earth and destroyed almost every person and animal, on the basis that we simply do not understand God and God's ways, is not an answer. It is smoke and mirrors or an answer that is a non-answer. It is an admission of ignorance and confusion. It says, "We don't understand." The alternative, or figurative interpretation, suggests truth is found in the fact the writer of the passage was dealing with deeper truth by using a parable. This must clearly be the case concerning the stories of creation. Another possibility is the writer believed the story of Noah to be true and was mistaken. After all, the case has been successfully made that some authors of scripture had false notions (see sermon Z-5, "Blemishes And Biblical Authentication"). In such a case, the Bible is still true in that the writer really believed what he (men for the most part) had written concerning God to be true. Old Testament writers actually believed God wanted the people to stone their children to death at one period in time (Leviticus 20:9). Of course, God never wanted such a thing; the truth lies in the fact that the writers believed it.

c. The puzzle. If there is both myth and factual history in our Bible, the problem is to distinguish between the two, which is necessary if we are to get at the truth. To begin, we must honestly admit that *no one*, not even the fundamentalists, takes the Bible literally in its entirety (see sermon O-5, "Nobody Actually Takes The Bible Literally"). Where do we draw the line: parable, myth, or history; fact or fiction? We could depend upon scholars; but that would only be removing our decision one step further, for the question then becomes, "Which scholars are the sound and sensible ones who are approaching their interpretation without prejudice, as opposed to the ones looking *for what they want to find*?" We may be left to common sense, and hope the differences are obvious. Good rational logic should be fairly dependable in differentiating between myth and history. We can try the reasonable tests of asking: Is this consistent with the loving nature of God revealed in Jesus? Is it congruous with God's laws of nature? Then we can ask the question: Is it verifiable? The life and ministry of Jesus is certainly authenticated by the different accounts in the gospels, which agree totally in their presentation of the nature and spirit of Jesus despite the contradictions in details (see sermon Z-5, "Blemishes And Biblical Authentication"). His life and resurrection made such a profound impact on history as to clearly validate its genuineness.

U-8. Putting Leftovers In The Offering Plate

Purpose Statement: *Do we give our best for God, or have we conveniently placed the church and our religion low on our list of priorities?*

Three ministers were talking about the way they handled the morning church offering. The Baptist said he drew a small circle on his office floor and threw the money from the offering plate into the air. What came down inside the circle he kept; what fell outside the circle belonged to God. The Presbyterian said she followed the same procedure, only reversed the allocation: what fell inside the circle was God's, and what fell outside was hers. The Methodist said her plan was similar: she threw the money into the air, God took what God wanted, and everything that fell to the floor belonged to the pastor. Everybody knows that Cain killed his brother, Abel. Few people know why. Each brought an offering to God: Cain, a farmer, brought *some* of his harvest to God; Abel, a rancher, brought the best or firstborn of his flocks for his offering. God said Abel's offering was better, and Cain became jealous (Genesis 4:1-7).
    a. God deserves our best. The Israelites were instructed by God to always offer their firstborn males as an offering: their animals as a burnt offering and their children to serve

God (Exodus 13:2, 11-12). The *first* fruits of their harvest, herds, flocks, or labor were to be dedicated to God. Offerings to God were so central and important in the worship of the Israelites that Leviticus and Numbers are largely given over to describing the kinds of offerings and the way they should be presented. Priests are to be very careful concerning the ritual procedure, the way they dress, and even concerning their own purification (Leviticus 22:1-3). Proverbs 3:9 stresses the need to present the very best of what the land produces, and it is a central theme of much of the Old Testament. Christians have justified building magnificent churches or lavish cathedrals in the spirit of giving only the best to God. This has occasionally been done even in areas of serious poverty, such as South America. We (used to) dress in our best clothes and make our worship formal and stately as an attempt to show reverence for God.

b. Is God getting our second best? Malachi makes a very pointed accusation (3:6-10) that the people are cheating or robbing God in the offering department. Is the message relevant for us today? Recall how Jesus visited the temple, observed what was going on, and became uncharacteristically angry. He drove the moneychangers and animal sellers out, calling them thieves. Part of the reason was because they had commercialized the house of worship (John 2:13-16). We have been told that part of the problem also was the scandal of the dealers forcing worshipers to exchange the gifts they brought, as inferior or imperfect, for perfect gifts provided by the moneychangers and animal vendors. God deserved only perfect animals, and of course the animals the worshipers brought from home for the burnt offering would be found to have blemishes. They would have to replace the defective animal with one of the vendor's perfect ones. Of course perfect animals would cost so much more than ordinary ones. God does not want burnt offerings from us today. However, if our reverence for God is serious, we should contribute only the best of our money, time, and talents. Where does worship and church work fall on our list of priorities? We can make it to Sunday morning services if company doesn't come. We will attend the Bible study sessions if they don't conflict with bowling night. We need to make a serious appraisal of where our faith and its responsibilities stand in our priorities.

U-9. Do You Ever Pretend To Be A Christian?

Purpose Statement: *How do we evaluate our own personal sincerity as we try to put our faith into action?*

When you were a child did you ever play pretend? Did you ever make-believe you were Wonder Woman or Superman? When you dressed up in a Halloween costume were you pretending to be some other character? If you were ever in the theatre or acted in school plays, in a sense you were pretending to be something other than you really are. The question you probably don't like to ask is, "Do you or I ever pretend to be a Christian?"

    a. Definition of a Christian. Consider two descriptions of what being a Christian entails. First is the popular definition: A Christian is a person who has accepted Jesus Christ as her or his personal savior. This seems sound and proper, but it always leaves me cold. I would prefer a more active definition than this one, one that seems less formula-like. It sounds like a pledge of allegiance that may become superficial. We are reminded of the story of the two sons (Matthew 21:28-31). One son told his father he would go and work in the field, but he didn't. The other son said he wouldn't work in the field, but he did. Jesus would have good reason for telling that story to us today as he might try to communicate the idea, "Talking the talk is not enough; you have to walk the walk." Jesus said not everyone who proclaimed him as Lord would be sincere. Honorableness is found in our words and *our actions* (Matthew 7:21). I prefer a definition of Christian as one who is sincerely trying to follow Jesus and honestly trying to do God's will. Notice, the operative word, *trying*. The implication is no one is perfect; and we all fall short. The important thing is that our efforts be earnest and real.

b. Definition of phony. According to Jesus, after our profession of faith, we may only go through the motions and still be a phony (Matthew 7:22-23). Jesus clearly described a religious phony when he attacked the Pharisees (Matthew 15:1-9), quoting Isaiah, who in turn speaking for God, said the people put on a good show, but their heart wasn't right. The most damning criticism Jesus leveled at the Pharisees (Matthew 23:13-28), though it was intended for the Jewish leaders, is quite applicable for some of us on occasions. We must be willing to apply the test of hypocrisy to our own religious lives. No doubt we try to fool "some of the people all of the time, and all of the people some of the time" with our Christian activities. Haven't we known people who seem so religious, while their piety seems hypocritical and phony? And while we *judge* them, they may be saying the very same thing about us.

c. Definition of sincerity. In one sense, all of us pretend to be Christians because we all try to act out the Christian life, even though we know we sometimes fail. There are times when it is appropriate to pretend to do the Christian thing though it is not the real us at the moment. When we are ill, tired, frustrated, depressed, angry, or upset and yet we are able to put on a Christian face and be a good witness to our faith, it is justifiable pretending. It depends on our motives. If we are trying to make the kind of Christian witness we know is proper so as to help others, or be a good influence or example — that's good. If we are pretending for self-glorification or personal advantage — that's bad. Motive is important, and attitude equally so. Paul says no matter what we do, it is only noise, commotion, and insignificance if we don't have love (1 Corinthians 13:1-3). Jesus adds humility and innocence to the mix (Matthew 18:1-5).

U-10. Our Cat Doesn't Know We Don't Have A Cat

Purpose Statement: *So many people don't realize they belong to God, and some of us that do realize it, still aren't aware of the many wonderful gifts God has given us.*

Did you ever have a stray cat come to your door and because you felt sorry for it you began to feed it? You let it be known you were not adopting it. What you didn't know was that you just became the proud owner of a new cat. Or more probably, what you didn't know was that the cat had become the proud owner of a new family. It is interesting to speculate on what reality is and how little of it we actually perceive. For example have you ever walked around with a "Kick me" sign on your back without knowing it? We hope we have not been a victim of the spinach-in-our-teeth-unaware embarrassment while conversing with others. They say what we don't know won't hurt us. That may or may not be true. However, we can say with conviction that some things we don't know are blessing us each day.

    a. Some don't know they are children of God. There are many persons running around in the world for whom God is only a concept, a vague idea about which they couldn't care less. Jesus made it a point to speak of God as a loving parent with whom we could communicate through prayer. Knowing we are created as special people by a loving eternal power in the universe gives us greater perspective, hope, more meaningful purpose, and directions for moral behavior. When we are ignorant of this we find our world floundering in pain and suffering through war, poverty, greed, and apathy.

    b. Some don't know they are beneficiaries of God's gifts daily. That elusive spark of life that scientists don't understand is the daily gift of existence. It is the breath we take; the beat of our hearts; the consciousness of our minds; it is the divine presence in our lives. The world is a delicately balanced eco-system providing everything necessary for life in every aspect: physical, mental, and spiritual. Scientists tell us that we have just the right amount of gravity, distance from the sun, atmosphere, mixture of chemical elements, and every resource to sustain life for millions of years. If any of a number of relationships were ever so slightly askew, life here, as we know it, could not continue. The earth floats through a vast void in tune with the universe. We may walk around generally oblivious to our dependence on God and God's great creation, and not be much more knowledgeable of our world and God than our cat is of its connection with our family.

c. Some don't know they are already saved. Because of the unbelievable forgiveness and love of God that Jesus revealed, I believe we are all "saved." Certainly we are all agreed that salvation is offered to every person on earth. Most of earth's inhabitants have hardly any idea of this fact. Most, even if they have heard of the concept of heaven or eternal life, take little solace or notice of this Easter revelation. Along with just being too busy to meditate on what lies beyond death, many people find it frightening or uncomfortable to contemplate.

Awareness of the full scope of the Christian message significantly enhances our appreciation for life, our universe, and the special gifts from God. This knowledge is necessary for us to ever have a world of peace and justice. What yet don't you know?

V.

V-1. "Feel Good" Religion: A Contemporary Theology

Purpose statement: *Has the trend in our religion or faith today deteriorated to the point where our churches are in danger of becoming simply a good time social-club experience?*

Since the '60s there seems to have been revitalization in religious interest and participation, but it also seems to be in a specific direction or following a definite pattern. Religious growth is found in new congregations springing up on the suburban edges of communities (and rarely found in inner cities or elsewhere in larger cities) and housed in buildings that look like schools. Often a sign out front is the only clue to the nature of the building as they generally shy away from obvious religious symbols and traditional church architecture, including the modern church architecture. The theology of the church, which will usually be conservative, is "good time" theology. It is intended to make the members happy, satisfied, and justified, in contrast to a "full gospel" theology, which does not just inspire and lift up, but also challenges and disturbs. Remember the prophets, the religious leaders of the Bible, and even Jesus seriously offended people. When we go to church we should expect to be inspired, comforted, and supported. However, we should also expect to have times when we don't like what we hear. If I understand what Jesus was really saying about possessions and wealth, among many other challenging ideas, I should be very uncomfortable. In contrast, the modern trend seems to be a one-dimensional message.

    a. What: Today's church experience is all about feeling good about yourself. "I'm okay, you're okay. God loves you and you are a good person. Your sins are forgiven, so just forget them. We won't talk about nasty issues that make you feel uncomfortable such as: capital punishment, racism, separation of church and state, and similar issues. We're saved; we will give others a chance to have our salvation if they will come to our church; if not, it's a shame. Those liberal churches are sending people to hell." Hiding behind this theology is an attitude suggesting that the unsaved deserve their unfortunate conditions. "The poor, the criminal, the unlikable, the liberal, and the unconventional created their own misery. Who knows, God may have predestined them to be lost. Who are we to second-guess God? If it were intended they should be saved, they would come to our church. We would make some of them welcome." These are the vibrations emanating from these churches, which are even beginning to influence the direction of the mainline churches.

b. Why: The pastor wants to be popular (and consequently needs to have a great personality), and must avoid all controversy and unpleasant topics. The secret is to appease the members so as not to lose any; we must maintain church growth. It helps when church members can feel they are in a very select or elite group knowing there are plenty of persons who are left out, and who deserve to be. We want to be assured that our many possessions are not sinful despite what Jesus may have said concerning materialism. As long as we go to church and take our loyalty oath to Jesus, proclaiming him a good guy, everything will be all right.

c. So: The church today may be in danger of losing its purpose and sense of mission. We should heed the danger of materialism and greed. We must not be paternalistically self-righteous nor be looking for a pat on the back validation of our salvation. There may be more honesty in our faith if we find our self squirming over the difficult demands of the Christian lifestyle — the authentic Christian way that resulted in the persecution of the first followers of Jesus.

For related scripture see Matthew 23:23-28.

V-2. Take This Religion Test

Purpose Statement: *Periodically, each pastor should challenge each of us with the question, "Are we making progress in our spiritual journey?"*

Even if it seems somewhat mechanical, the evaluation, planning, and the follow-through involved in our review of our personal spiritual life progress, such a review is necessary. It is easy to stagnate or to believe that our faith is doing just fine. Our religious life can become habitual, which is not all bad as long as it maintains a meaning and intensity. Paul (Philippians 3:12-16) acknowledges he is not perfect and is diligently striving toward the goal, which should be our objective, also. To measure the progress of our personal faith journey, we need to give ourselves a simple religious test: "Are we better today than we were one year ago?" Is our relationship with God, our understanding of Jesus, and our love for others greater than it used to be? It remains true that we either make progress or we backslide; there is no standing still. We shouldn't be misled by the childlike or simple nature of such a test of our progress. Consider how easily one loses enthusiasm, or forgets one's Christian mission.

a. Taking the test. How do we go about taking our spiritual temperature? Is it too mechanical to check our church attendance, daily meditations, and the amount of financial support or personal time we give in service? Perhaps to more effectively evaluate our spiritual progress, stepping back and taking an honest look may involve a "spiritual retreat" with a group or alone in our own private "get away."

b. Making a new plan. Honest and perceptive evaluation is difficult, but necessary. Setting goals might be the easiest step. Consistent and faithful follow-through requires serious preparation. Where should we be as Christians in our spiritual journey?

c. Getting started. This is where the church can offer more encouragement. Support groups in the church could include Sunday school and other classes, formal retreat-like fellowships as well as the casual and on-going caring of the congregation.

d. Taking the test again. The best motivator will be periodic checkups, and again this can be done best with a spiritual small group or retreat "reunion." Such an experience every so often where we worship and fellowship together, and "take the test" again fuels the fire for the journey in the cycle of progress.

V-3. Could Uncle Tom Be A Christ Figure?

Purpose Statement: *It could be possible many Christians are unappreciative of the significance of the "Christ figure."*

We think we know Jesus very well. Yet it remains possible we still "don't get it" when it comes to the magnitude of Jesus' love, and how each of us is called to live a life of such unconditional compassion. To understand the implications may be frightening. Attempts in literature to portray just what would be entailed in being a "Christ figure" in our day (or contemporary of the particular author) probably are accurate when they represent the masses as totally misunderstanding Jesus. Arguably, the Christ image in some of Dostoevsky's heroes, Prince Nekhludov in Leo Tolstoy's *Resurrection*, or other fictional characters, fails to capture the full essence of Jesus. However, my assessment is Uncle Tom in *Uncle Tom's Cabin* is the most accurate Christ figure in fiction. This certainly won't be a popular view. Very possibly, if we truly understood him, Jesus would seem offensive to most persons today, even to many Christians. He offended the religious leaders of his own day.

I believe Uncle Tom may be the best role model of Jesus we have in fiction. (Apart from this theme, the novel itself is considered by many to have been the most powerful instrument to encourage abolition of slavery in its day.) Uncle Tom's behavior exemplifies what it means to follow Jesus in an almost perfect way.

African-Americans have legitimate criticisms of the novel when they are offended by the language and attitudes portrayed in its historical setting. In addition, one could argue the author, as a white person, was not in a position to understand the black experience. Nevertheless, Harriet Beecher Stowe understood Jesus, and Uncle Tom became her very perceptive rendition of how to live as a Christian under the most terrible of circumstances. Uncle Tom was:

    a. Consecrated. He understood Jesus and dedicated his life faithfully to follow Jesus. He could not hurt (and certainly never kill) anyone. He would face his own death before inflicting suffering upon any other person, and did die because he refused to harm another. He remained faithful to his Christian faith even unto death.

    b. Compassionate. The love of Jesus was even for his enemies; he forgave them as they killed him on the cross. Tom showed Christian love for the cruelest of slave owners and overseers; not in the sense of affection, but rather in the sincere desire for only good will for them. Like Jesus he was willing to sacrifice his own life even for his enemies. This is the "foolishness for Christ" that Paul talked about (1 Corinthians 1:18-31; 4:10-13), and that many of us Christians still have trouble accepting.

    c. Courageous. Unfortunately, Uncle Tom has become synonymous with a doormat or spinelessness. This could not be farther from the truth. He manifested the greatest courage one could possibly show when he willingly died before he would inflict suffering on another slave! In our day, Uncle Tom would be a powerful non-violent activist for civil rights. Uncle Tom was a man of the greatest convictions, ultimate love, and unbelievable courage. The world suffers much tragedy and violence today because it simply does not comprehend that kind of godliness, and does not have enough Uncle Toms!

Suggested passages might include John 18:10-11, 36 and Romans 5:6-11 among many possibilities.

V-4. Knowing What To Know

Purpose Statement: *Theology and religion encompass the totality of life and are so all-inclusive that we are unable to know everything. Consequently, the question is, "What is it important for us to know and what should be peripheral to our knowledge?"*

Formerly, people knew their Bible much better than we do today. But what did they know and was it the right knowledge? There used to be a greater emphasis on memorizing Bible passages. But what "version" would you use to memorize today?

Many fundamentalists or conservative Christians will memorize biblical passages or "pat" answers to certain set questions that they might encounter in a dialogue with the lost or unsaved, that they might argue effectively with them. Many Christians memorize or know those favorite passages that they have discovered to be uplifting and inspirational. Nevertheless, it is important to know just what things we should know and what things are not important to know.

    a. Don't need to know. Simple facts such as the names of Jesus' disciples, where Nicodemus lived, or how many "chosen" will be saved from the twelve tribes seems irrelevant (although simple biblical usage will make us familiar with a great deal of unimportant trivia). We should ask ourselves, "How relevant and practical is this or that passage of scripture? Is it helpful to know; will it make a difference in my life and my ethical decisions, or is it useless information?" One apocryphal story (1 Infancy 20:1-8) tells of Jesus' teacher leading him through his *ABC*'s. He asks Jesus the first letter of the alphabet. Jesus says, "Aleph." The teacher asks him to name the second. Jesus replies, "First, tell me the meaning of Aleph before we go on to Beth." The point is that we shouldn't waste time learning useless facts or gathering information that will not be useful. A pastor once asked me what I thought of the __th commandment. Since I did not have the "numbers" of the commandments memorized, I had to confess I had no idea what commandment he was talking about, thereby exposing my biblical ignorance. Had he identified the commandment as concerned with stealing, killing, or adultery, I could have shared my carefully worked out opinions. As it was, "I didn't know my Bible." Had I tried to explain the essence of this sermon to him, he may not have understood. We should learn to recognize trivia and the irrelevant and pass quickly over it to the meaningful.

b. Do need to know. The Bible is intended to provide help in finding answers to critical questions concerning life, revelation of the nature of God, knowledge related to ethical decisions, and inspirational scripture. We need to become immersed in the teachings of Jesus in order to become appropriate Christian witnesses, understand the meaning of salvation, develop meaningful relationships with others, live righteous and moral lives, and so much more. We must spend our time getting to know the significant and relevant.

For related scripture see Proverbs 1:1-6; 8:1-10; or Sirach 6:18-37 (Apocrypha).

V-5. God Needs An Alias

Purpose Statement: *We have become very lax concerning "taking God's name in vain," as well as the name of Jesus, and we need to focus on what this means regarding our respect for God and Jesus.*

There have been periods in our Bible history when people were afraid to speak God's name, "God," or whatever it happened to be at that point in time. The reason for this was that God was so great and should be revered above all else. We were too lowly to be permitted to say the name of God, as it would constitute a disrespectful familiarity with God. It would be analogous to situations when it is considered disrespectful for children to call adults by their first names. Thus they must say "Mr. Cain" and not "Terry." Over the years, even though I requested church members to call me by my first name, some only felt comfortable calling me "Reverend Cain" or "Doctor Cain." In turn, I found it difficult when I first began serving churches to call the elderly members, Jenny, Ruth, and Carl as they requested me to do. I was steeped in the tradition of Mr., Miss, or Mrs. for my elders. On one occasion I heard someone refer to a pastor by his first name, only to have the pastor's wife respond (in a cold, serious tone), "Please call my husband Reverend _____."

During the biblical periods we are talking about, to avoid saying God's name, the people would select another term as a substitute. However, that "new name" would soon become too familiar and thus "disrespectful," or else the euphemism would finally seem to become God's real name, and another "substitute" name would be needed. Over time, God has had many names: El, Elohim, El-elyon, El Shaddai, and Yahweh (Jehovah). Not all names for God were for the reason cited above; some were because of changes in language and tradition. Another example of the ineffable names for God was "Adonai." Appropriate scripture would be the third commandment (Deuteronomy 5:11 and Exodus 20:7). Exodus 3:13-14, where Moses inquires about God's name and is told it is "I Am," offers possibilities.

    a. It is true we're careless with God's name. From one extreme of not being appropriate to speak God's name, today we often encounter the other extreme: The names of God and Jesus are used as slang and cursing. So many of us use the expression, "Oh, my God!" not as a prayer or religiously, but as a careless slang expression. Recently on television I heard one of the actors say in anger, "for Christ's sake." Again, this was not done religiously. Parallel to finding substitutes for "God" because God's name has become too familiar as mentioned above, there is the modern phenomenon of finding euphemisms for "God" or "Jesus" to avoid abusing those words in slang or cursing. Thus we have corrupted the words with "jeez," "gee whiz," "golly," "gol' darn it," "dag nab it," "doggone it," "jimminy cricket," and a host of others as a veiled attempt to avoid using the names, "God" or "Jesus," more directly.

b. It hurts our relationship with God. Of course the flippant use of God's and Jesus' names, or substitutes for their names, does not diminish God or Jesus. However, there is no question that it erodes our respect and reverence. It creates an attitude of casualness toward or concerning God and Jesus. Or possibly, it may be the other way around: The attitudes we develop are finally expressed in the way we trivialize the names of God and Jesus.

c. It becomes a denigrating witness to others. When we use such expressions and attitudes in the presence of other persons, it creates an atmosphere of serious disrespect for that which is holy. In a word, it is blasphemy.

How much does our choice of words indicate our feelings and attitudes about God?

V-6. It's The Least You Can Do

Purpose Statement: *What is the minimum expected behavior for a Christian?*

Amidst the lofty expectations and rigorous discipline that we Christians consider part of proper Christian behavior, could there be some simple basic requirements that would constitute the minimum we could expect of every Christian? These actions or attitudes would be the lowest common denominator for Christian behavior. To be a disciple of Jesus means to "take up our cross" and "make sacrifices." Do the little amenities — the least we can do — get lost in the grander scheme of things? A Christian should not steal, lie, or cheat. A Christian should give generously, serve faithfully for Christ, and love others, including enemies. However, we may occasionally neglect the more subtle acts and attitudes. One scripture to consider is Luke 17:7-10 (an interesting parable concerning doing our duty), or the two parables in Luke 13:18-21 (the mustard seed and the yeast).

When Jesus scolded the Pharisees (Matthew 23:23-24), he suggested they were faithful in little things, but failed to do the more important things. Our concern seems to be the opposite. Consider these three simple examples of the least a Christian should do.

    a. Smile. A Christian should remember to be friendly. Some people on the streets will greet you; most will not. There seems to be an inverse ratio of the number of people and the chances of a friendly greeting. On the streets of a busy city, few, if any, will give you a smile or say, "Hello." A friendly greeting is more likely to occur in a small town, and when you are out in the wilderness hiking and where you seldom pass another person on the trail, when you do meet someone, inevitably they will greet you. You feel good when someone smiles and says a friendly word to you. A lot of folks could use such a greeting. Even though they may not return the greeting (being caught unaware, perhaps), it will mean something to them and perhaps they will pass it on to the next person they meet. I have noticed that it is easier to greet some people than others. Unfortunately, another's appearance may determine whether we offer a smile or not. Probably, the very person we don't greet is the one most in need of a friendly greeting and vice versa.

    b. Back off. Being independent people of privilege we may barge through life expecting others to make room for us. Courtesy requires of us (and Christianity demands) behavior that considers the needs and feelings of every other person. We should back up and let the other person go first, and say, "Excuse or pardon me," "I'm sorry," or "May I be of help?" Every contact with another is an opportunity to serve Christ and show Christian love, even in the little ways.

    c. Clean up. There are those among us who, when passing through a parking lot or down the street and coming upon litter, will pick it up and put it in a trash receptacle near by. There is so much litter we can't pick it all up, but a little every now and then makes some difference. An additional upside is that others may see our act and begin to do it themselves, or at least, perhaps our actions may cause a few others who observe us to stop littering.

What are other ways that you can suggest that are the least we Christians can do to be loving and considerate?

V-7. Who Do You Love Better: God Or Me?

Purpose Statement: *What does it mean to love God more than your spouse or parent or child?*

Honest Christians (a redundancy) admit they are perplexed by some statements Jesus made regarding our love for God in comparison with our affection for loved ones and friends. Jesus said that we are not worthy of being his followers unless we love him more than we love our mother and father, spouse, and children (Luke 14:26). By any standard, that is a very strong statement. He also said that the first commandment is to love God with everything (Luke 10:27), and the second commandment is to love your neighbor as yourself. Many of us could confess that we love our family, perhaps even our friends, better than God and Jesus. If so, we probably feel guilty about it, and this sermon is warranted. To begin with, it is proper to interpret "love your neighbor" as including family and friends.

    a. Loving Jesus. We might interpret "loving Jesus more" to mean loving him is pledging our loyalty to a "way of life" or God's will. This "way of life" means giving our unconditional love to others, including our loved ones. We do our utmost to serve them by this "way of life" in doing everything for their best interest. This will mean that occasionally loving our family and friends will result in doing something for their own good they may not agree with or understand — just as a parent will do what is in the best interest for their child even though the child doesn't agree. Jesus could have also intended us to understand that by loving him we really love God.

    b. Loving God. This idea is more abstract. We know God, and yet we do not see God physically apart from God's creation. To love God, whom we do not see, is far different from loving our family. Both include desire for a relationship, forgiveness, comfort, and support in difficulties, and so forth. They differ in that we "do for" our loved ones, willing what is best "for" our loved ones. We don't "will the best" for God who is perfect and almighty and doesn't need our help, except for serving, loving, and willing the best for others. Loving God may be more intellectual and abstract, and not as emotional in contrast to loving others, which will be more emotional and not as abstractly intellectual. Loving God is reverence for life in totality. Loving parent, child, or friend is distinctively individual and more personal.

c. Loving others. This is more concrete and easier to understand and visualize. We know how to love our family and friends. But can we love others, such as our neighbor (even our enemies), as much as our loved ones? Can we actually love others as much as we do ourselves? As far as emotional ties, we can never love strangers as much as we love family. However, we can love all persons in the sense that we actively will the very best for everyone without prejudice. Can we love others as much as we love ourselves? Let us remind ourselves that people have been able to give up their lives for others — even strangers.

d. Which takes precedence? To return to an old analogy, which is more important to our life: our brain or our heart? Loving God is to love others. True love for others is loving God. We cannot love God and not love others. This explains the words of Jesus that "loving your neighbor," is the same as "loving God with everything" (Matthew 22:37-39).

For related scripture see 1 John 4:7-21.

V-8. The Ubiquitous Nature Of Religion

Purpose Statement: *Christians need to be reminded that religion or theology undergirds and encompasses all of life.*

Without disturbing or distorting the typical definition of religion as relating to our beliefs concerning God and our worship of God, we could make the claim that religion involves everything, all of life. One of the best expressions of our topic is Psalm 139. It reminds us that God is always with us: there is nowhere we may flee from God. This is a reality whether or not we are aware of it or admit it. Everything belongs to the Creator and must relate to the Creator.

   a. We cannot escape God. One can claim to be an atheist and claim all religion as foolishness. This would be tantamount to saying I am not a person and there is no world. Bishop Berkeley said there is no real material world; it is all in our finite minds and in the form of God's infinite mind. He may say whatever he philosophically pleases; you and I know the universe is more than smoke and mirrors. Similarly, the atheist's position is like the ventriloquist's dummy giving no credence to its creator or the ventriloquist. God created us, sustains all life, and is an inescapably part of us as Psalm 139 clearly states.
   b. Religion is our posture toward life. One cannot say there isn't any religion or philosophy, for that position itself is only one form of religion or philosophy. It is not for us to say we will have none of religion for religion is our stance, our philosophy, our belief about our self and our world. We must necessarily deal with our existence and our environment, as we must breathe the air whether we believe in air or not. It is not a matter of accepting or rejecting. It is only a matter of what we will believe as our religion regardless of its approximation to the truth. Our beliefs may be close to the truth or very misguided; but we have a religion.

c. Religion dominates the universe. It will determine our moral choices, our lifestyles, and our interactions with our environment, as the inescapable umbrella to our total existence. This explains why we hear it said we should avoid religion and politics as topics of conservation so as to eliminate controversy. These subjects are fraught with complexities and emotions as they touch the very heart of being. This also explains why so many people with emotional and mental problems focus on the religious. Again, it is because it is at the heart of life and speaks to everything. It determines how we view the world and act in it.
d. So what? Can you yet ask what is the point of all this? It means religion is concerned with all of life. This means sermons can address every concern. When the subject of our preaching is acceptable to some listeners, for them it is a great sermon. When the same subject is objectionable to other listeners, for them the minister had no business preaching on that topic. We can no longer afford to place religion and theology to one side as just another discipline as if it were one of the classes in school we may choose or choose not to take. The point is, since it is unavoidable, we must stop running away from our faith and its application to every part of our lives. What are you going to do with it?

V-9. Catch Me If You Can

Purpose Statement: *A congregation should be invited into dialogue with the minister regarding the sermons.*

(Warning: "do not try this at home" or church, unless you are ready to receive criticism.) If daring enough, the minister can challenge the congregation to challenge him or her by encouraging extensive feedback on his or her preaching. While this could be very uncomfortable and even lead to hurt feelings, it could be a tremendous growing experience. This could be conversation from the pew in a talkback during the message, though time and purpose would dictate a longer separate session of evaluation and discussion on another occasion. Church members may find this difficult, and not feel free and comfortable doing this. However, if we would like to improve our preaching, we can prompt the listeners what to watch for in the messages that would help the pastor know how he or she is doing. Second Corinthians 10 is one example where Paul mentions criticism he has received, and proceeds to defend himself. The biggest obstacle we may encounter in encouraging feedback from the congregation is finding the response quite disturbing. Instead of shedding light and initiating any helpful change, we could become defensive and try to justify what we said and how we said it. Of course, the majority of those sitting in the pew are not experts in either theology or homiletics. Yet, if there are any problems in communications, the pastor is the person that must deal with them. This sermon would encourage such evaluation and alert the member as to what to look for. A few of the possible concerns to note could include:

a. Variety. One of the biggest criticisms I have as I visit churches and listen to Sunday morning preaching is that it is too often the same sermon preached over and over: a different tune, but the same lyrics. It sounds like this: "We need to get right with God and things will be better." Hopefully this book of message ideas has avoided such a narrow focus. It is essential for the minister to cover all the bases and deal with the full range of critical questions and issues church members need to struggle with.

b. Consistency. Are there any glaring contradictions (or even sneaky ones) in the message or all of the messages in aggregate? Sensitive listeners may ferret out such irregularities and bring them to the minister's attention.

c. Clarity. This ranks right up at the top with the first point, "variety," as one of the biggest concerns with our preaching. Such a simple question as, "What did the preacher say today?" can be most embarrassing. It is all about communication no matter how wonderful the message may be. Don't they tell a story about our president, Coolidge, coming home from Sunday services and being asked what the preacher's message was about? He answered, "Sin." He was asked what the preacher said about sin. His answer was, "He's agin' it." Can they even say that much about our sermons?

d. Accuracy. Of course, it is necessary that our facts and figures are straight. But far more critical is the need to have our theology be right. This is the most frightening aspect of preaching; because every preacher believes he or she has the truth; the sermons in one community alone may run the gamut of extremes. We are dealing with people's lives, their emotions, and their spiritual well-being. A congregation talkback and sermon evaluation could be most helpful in this area of concern, but, unfortunately, this is also the arena where the congregation is sometimes least equipped for healthy and helpful dialogue. Could we be distorting God's truth in any of our messages?

A sermon introducing this possibility to the congregation is a must if the pastor can handle it. Such an exercise would benefit pastor and church member. The parishioners will have more exciting and better sermons to hear, and they would become conditioned to give more thoughtful attention to, and evaluation of, the message.

V-10. Hell: But, It's A Dry Heat

Purpose Statement: *From biblical information and what we know of the nature of God, what should we understand to be the nature of "hell"?*

Everyone has seen the poster or T-shirt with the dehydrated or skeleton-like person crawling across the desert with the caption, "But, it is a dry heat." In other words, is the heat of "hell" accurately understood by most of us, and is it possibly not as bad as portrayed in scripture? We are familiar with the "old-time fire and brimstone" preaching where the point is to frighten us into accepting Jesus by vivid descriptions of an eternity of fiery torture. Actually this technique is not all that "old-time" as some preachers still excitedly expound such images. However, I believe that hell's bark is worse than its bite. Perhaps, I will be rudely surprised concerning my mistaken theology about one minute after I die, and some Christians may have already assigned me to a destination that involves a devil, some pitchforks, and not a small amount of fire. Hopefully, it will be a dry heat. How can we possibly accept the hate and fear associated with some folk's image of hell? Out of a plethora of possible ideas concerning hell, here are a few that seem pertinent.

    a. It is not a place. More likely it is a spiritual experience where we struggle with our remorse over the sins we have committed. In a just universe, we would expect consequences for decisions of a hurtful and offensive nature toward ourselves and others. Justice dictates repercussions for our thoughts and actions. If we understand hate and violence, it necessarily follows they will breed depression and remorse, just as love will bring peace and joy. Such consequences would seem to be built into the universe's spiritual laws. Such an arrangement seems to fit with the comments Jesus made concerning hell as weeping and crying and gnashing of teeth in outer darkness (Matthew 8:12; 22:13; 25:30).

    b. It is ruled by love. God is not a monster who would condemn people (it is suggested even good people whose only significant mistake is not accepting Jesus) to eternal punishment. As Henry Fielding says in his novel, *The Adventures of Joseph Andrews*, "For can anything be more derogatory to the honor of God, than for men to imagine that the all-wise Being will hereafter say to the good and virtuous, 'Notwithstanding the purity of thy life, notwithstanding that constant rule of virtue and goodness in which you walked upon earth, still as thou didst not believe everything in the true orthodox manner, thy want of faith shall condemn thee?' " To believe in such a monster is to not understand all that Jesus said about a loving parent God, or what is so eloquently expressed about God's love in 1 John 4:7-21. God does not motivate us or call us out of fear of hell, but reaches out to us in love causing us to respond to that love. Any biblical allusions to a frightening hell of eternal torment must be attributed to the cultural exaggeration form of emphasis used by Jesus and those of his day (see sermon Q-6, "Would Jesus Stretch The Truth?"). For example: camels through needle's eyes, a log or beam in your eye, swallowing a camel, moving mountains, and giving everything to the poor. Our sins will entail some sorrow, suffering, and repentance, but it is neither unbearable torture nor eternal.

c. It is for everyone. An intriguing possibility is that there is not a heaven and hell, but an everlasting spiritual existence where we continue our spiritual struggle, either to grow or regress in our relationship with God and others. Perhaps we enter such an existence at the level dictated by our spiritual attainment in this life and continue on in our development from that point. This opens the door to a possible "universal salvation" where God is never ultimately defeated in the desire for all of God's children to be "saved." This would be consistent with the nature of our loving God and the theology expressed in the teachings of Jesus: the eleventh hour workers, prostitutes, and tax gatherers getting to heaven before the good people, and so forth. Discounting some biblical cultural exaggerations in descriptions and allowing for the style of emphasis Jesus used, such a scenario is not really unbiblical.

d. It begins here and now. In our more sensitive moments, our remorse over moral failures and social indiscretions causes us serious depression, guilt feelings, anxiety, and hurt in this life. Is this a taste of hell or perhaps the heaven/hell experience actually begins here and now and continues beyond death?

W.

W-1. Finding Your Way From Nazareth To Jerusalem

Purpose Statement: *So much of the Bible story involves geography, that a sermon on becoming familiar with the territory seems appropriate.*

Start by making copies of hand-out maps as inserts to the bulletin. It could be one or more maps, but they should be rather simple and uncluttered. Only the prime geographic features should be included. If more than one map is used, it should include a larger map that shows Egypt and the Tigris/Euphrates region, a map of the "Holy Land" which depicts Galilee and Judea, and a map of Paul's journeys. It could turn into a series of sermons.
  a. Point out the major geographic features that figure prominently in Bible history: major cities, Dead and Galilean Seas, Babylon, Ur, Jordan River, key mountains, and so forth.
  b. Tie the historic movements of the peoples to the land: the Babylonian captivity, the sojourn in Egypt, Paul's travels, Jesus' ministry, and similar events.
  c. Relate biblical ideas to geography: national relationships and ethnicity, enemies, chosen people, allies, Samaritans, other religions, or the Holy Land as strategic crossroads.

Scripture could include passages where knowledge of geography would be helpful.

W-2. Preaching To The Choir

Purpose Statement: *Are our assumptions accurate regarding church members (and non-church people) and their spiritual state, and are our sermons appropriate for our audience?*

We could assume the choir, as in "preaching to the choir," is a euphemism for church members as opposed to those "outside" of the church. It is not easy to know where various members of a congregation are in their spiritual journey, nor for that matter where people might be who have no relationship to a church. No doubt, this is one of the reasons why Jesus cautioned us to "judge not." Yet we, as pastors, who are called upon every Sunday to deliver sermons, need to know what we should be saying and to whom. What kind of sermons do most of us need to hear — no, really hear? Two of the more interesting letters found among the seven in Revelation are to the churches at Sardis and Laodicea (Revelation 3:1-6, 14-22). It seems that the faith had cooled in these two churches. Because their enthusiasm had waned, they needed a jump-start to revitalize their engines. The same seemed to be true concerning the letter to the Hebrews. Their once vital religion had grown old and worn out and needed rekindling (as in Hebrews 5:11—6:12). This may be a description of many congregations or individual church members today. Are there some erroneous assumptions we are all making about the "choir?"

    a. The preacher's assumption. The preacher may be wrong in assuming the "choir" does not need to be preached to. There may be two parts to the general foundation that underlies our messages. First, we need an initial experience with Jesus Christ and a relationship with God. Second, there is the ongoing growing stage of our spiritual progress (Hebrews 5:12). Every Sunday some preachers will dwell on messages that sound as if they were intended for the "unchurched" who aren't present. On the other hand, perhaps that is the word many of us still need to hear.

    b. The choir's assumption. The folks in the pew may be assuming they have "arrived" and don't need "preaching to." How many church members are listening to sermons while saying to themselves, "I wish those folks outside the church (and some inside, but not me) could hear this, they need it"? It is good to be reminded that Jesus preached his meanest and toughest sermons to the religious leaders of his day. He was preaching to the choir. He was preaching to the preachers as well.

c. Both assumptions could be wrong. We must not assume the "unchurched" need to hear the word more than we do. Jesus made some interesting comments concerning this subject. "Not everyone who claims Jesus as Lord is necessarily saved" (Matthew 7:21-23). "Prostitutes and tax collectors will go to heaven before us good folks" (Matthew 21:31). And not because they will die first. "The first shall be last and the last first" (Matthew 20:16). "Can we religious people see the speck in someone's else's eye beyond the large obstruction in our own?" (Matthew 7:3-5). The Samaritan clearly understood God's love more than the priest and Levite (Luke 10:30-37). The "great feast" parable (Luke 14:15-24) contains similar implications. The story of the two sons seems to follow this theme (Matthew 21:28-31). Our assumption that we are saved and others are lost should be carefully re-examined. The frightening truth is that many non-churched people sometimes act more like Christians than do Christians.

W-3. Should The Universe Make Sense — And Why?

Purpose Statement: *Are we meant to know some of the answers to the more significant questions concerning our world, or should our world remain a mystery?*

How often have we been told that some event was God's will when it seemed very improbable, or it was terribly inconsistent with the loving nature of God to do such a thing? If we question God's involvement, will we be told we are not meant to understand God's ways? Granted the universe is very complex: Physicists and astronomers are saying the universe at both extremes (on the very small scale and the very large scale) does not seem to operate as expected according to Newtonian laws. (Perhaps the answer is simply that we are still unable to measure accurately on those extreme levels that encompass the infinitesimally tiny and invisible particles, as well as the intergalactic structure stretching across billions of light years.) So also, some of the theological questions are complex and challenge our understanding. The question, "Should the universe make sense?" seems appropriate, as does the follow-up question, "Why?" These questions involve God and God's creation.

    a. Should the universe make sense?
        1. No, not in every sense or detail. It is too vast and wonderful. Just as we are confused and find the physical universe mystifying at both extremes of the size continuum, the spiritual universe will continue to confound us concerning a variety of questions. The physical concept of infinite space has its parallel in the theological concept of eternal life. These ideas are too big for our minds. We cannot comprehend life after death, how it can be and what it is like. Even the idea of God is too staggering for our limited minds.
        2. On the other hand, yes, our universe should make sense. While much mystery remains, still we know so much about our universe, and what we know fits together in a beautiful way following consistent physical laws. Again, paralleling the physical world, our spiritual universe of laws and truth makes sense the more we explore and investigate. For example, Jesus taught us to be meek, turn the other cheek, and return love to those who threaten or harm us. At first, this seems foolish. However, for those who have spent the time to get to know God, and have understood and practiced the teachings of Jesus, they find such an ethic works.
    b. If the universe should make sense, then why?
        1. One way in which it is important for the universe to make sense physically and spiritually is that in doing so it becomes dependable and encouraging. We do not live physically and spiritually in a universe that is capricious. It can be trusted. It is reliable. We can count on God's will and way when we have understood it. For example, we need it for our hope and assurance of life after death. Without such hope, this world would

be too cruel and vicious. There has to be compensation for the world's misery and injustice.
2. Another reason why the universe must make sense is for our moral direction. Only when the spiritual laws are understood are we able to function in their framework. It is then that we can say the teachings of Jesus and revelation of God are reasonable and consistent. We are able to understand them enough to know how we should respond.

Two suggested scripture passages: In John 8:32 Jesus tells us that knowing the truth makes us free. Proverbs 8:22-36 (among many other relevant Proverb passages) speaks about a beautiful truth or wisdom serving as the framework for the universe. It is logical, reasonable, spiritual, and physical law that is truth and knowledge. Proverbs makes it clear that without it we flounder and fail. With it we "find life" and "enjoy the universe."

W-4. Neither Peacock Nor Worm

Purpose Statement: *On finding the delicate balance between pride and humility.*

Isaiah 6:1-7 relates the story of Isaiah's religious experience in the temple, which makes him feel lowly and unworthy. He has just experienced the presence of God, and he recognizes how sinful he is and even how everything he says is sinful. It is only when his sins are forgiven, using the symbolic act of hot coals searing his lips, that he feels worthy to serve God. In Luke 14:7-11, Jesus advises us to always take the humble seat by the kitchen door at a dinner party. We may be invited up on the dais later. We are not to take one of the honored seats on our own or we may be embarrassed by being asked to step down to a more humble place. Jesus says when we think ourselves great, we will be humbled; when we humble ourselves, we will find respect. Psalm 8 is a beautiful description of the proper ego. Verse 4 speaks of the lowly place we humans occupy in a vast and wonderful universe. On the other hand, verse 5 says, "Yet we have been crowned with glory and honor," and only a little less important than angels. We need to examine the way we feel about ourselves, and then consider how we act upon that assessment. Each of us probably falls into one of the following three classifications.

    a. The arrogant. Some of us think very highly of ourselves, and consider ourselves better than others. Arrogant and overbearing people reeking with self-conceit are not pleasant to be around. In the scripture cited above from Luke 14, Jesus said people who consider themselves better than others will be in for a surprise and an embarrassment. "Pride goeth before a fall" (Proverbs 11:2; 16:18; 29:23; and 1 Timothy 3:6) is another way of saying, "Having a 'big head' invites a humiliation just as an inflated balloon tempts a poke with a pin." A few athletes and other celebrities have let public acclaim and fame make them obnoxious, which may partially explain why some famous sports stars get into trouble with the law. Arrogance leads us to believe we have special privileges. Romans 12:3 reminds us not to think too highly of ourselves, but to be modest and humble.

    b. Those with low self-esteem. Unfortunately, there are people with low self-esteem, who feel poorly about themselves and ashamed of who they are. This is tragic and unnecessary. We seldom feel sorry for the arrogant (we should); we just consider them jerks, while those with low self-esteem, we often pity. Being ashamed of who we are leads to an unhappy life at best, and in extreme cases may result in deep depression and even suicide.

    c. The modest person with self-respect. Feelings about one's self, extend along a continuum from arrogance (people who strut like peacocks), to feelings of worthlessness (the worms), and all degrees in between. As in so many instances the ideal is to find the happy medium or balance (see sermon Z-6, "A Dangerous Way To Read Your Bible") where we have a proper kind of pride or sense of dignity and worth, and yet remain modest and humble. Jesus taught us to appreciate how valuable we are, and how God loves us as children of God. We are special and wonderful. We are also sinners and should not consider ourselves better than others. God loves us all the same, because you and I were created in God's image.

W-5. Will Reverend Tortoise Ever Catch Doctor Hare?

Purpose Statement: *Is there a gap between science and ethics and what are we going to do about it?*

This science/ethics gap is an old idea containing much truth, and little seems to be done about it. We stand in awe of the wonders in scientific achievement. What has been accomplished in space exploration, the medical field, industrial and communications technology, and in the various other sciences, along with the entertainment industry, leaves us breathless. The classic fantasy is to imagine what kind of shock a person living in the 1800s, or earlier, would experience if suddenly thrown into today's amazing world. We have grown up exposed to this unbelievable world gradually, and consequently may take much of it for granted, failing to appreciate the wonder of it all. We simply take the telephone for granted and think nothing of the fantastic phenomenon that occurs each time we use the phone. It staggers my simple mind. There is no way I can speak into the phone in my home and communicate with someone 2,000 miles across the country almost instantaneously. It can't happen; it is impossible. My voice can't travel through that little wire to a point where it is transferred to invisible waves in the air till it reaches another point where it enters a little wire and finally into someone's home where they recognize my voice, all in less than a second. I don't believe it, but apparently it happens. The embarrassing question is, "Has there been *any* — let alone comparable — advance in ethical understanding or behavior over the same expanse of time?" We have created unbelievably efficient weapons to kill each other. At the same time, how much progress have we made in personal and international relationships? We expend great energy and billions of dollars for weapons, spy networks, weapon detection devices, homeland security, and for a war that kills and maims children in Iraq; all because we are not mature enough to know how to live in peace together.

This science/ethics gap can cause scientific achievements to become useless, wasteful, or dangerous. Do we really need to spend more money on a high-resolution television when my picture is beautiful now? There are homeless people in our own community and children in our world dying of hunger. Should we be using radioactive or nuclear energy until we have found a safe disposal method? Medical technology confronts us with serious ethical questions and we are not keeping pace. Suddenly, 1 Corinthians 13 reminds us everything is "noisy gongs and clanging bells" if there is no love. We are still looking into "mirrors when it is time to see face to face." It is time to replace childish thinking with mature responsibility. In the race for Reverend Tortoise (religion) to catch up with Doctor Hare (science), three questions come to mind.

    a. Why is there a gap? Probably for several reasons, which would include at least the following: First, if there is a chance to make more money, we'll do whatever it takes. Second, we have an obsession with gadgetry and the latest fads. Third, we selfishly want science to create a world of comfort, ease, and luxury for ourselves. Consequently, we continue to create conditions that need the moral direction we haven't mastered yet.

    b. Why don't we care? Until something affects us directly, we aren't motivated to care. When it gets around to affecting us, it is usually too late. At that point, finding answers is very difficult. It is more fun and exciting to have new wonder toys and convenient technology than it is to pursue ethical discussions.

    c. What can we do? First, we become informed about the issues. Next, our church can conduct groups and workshops regarding how we might apply our religion to those issues. Finally, there will be a time for action to share our information and encourage serious change in the way we currently do business, using letter writing, protests, and so forth.

W-6. It's Time To Quit

Purpose Statement: *Many or all of us have some things over which we need to get control. How do we do this?*

What are the bad habits and wasteful activities we want to conquer, ones that are costly and harmful? Some of us are losing the battle with these problems which range from drug and gambling addictions to smoking, not exercising, overeating, using alcohol, excessive preoccupation with sex, and addiction to games and internet activities. Some activities are not harmful in themselves such as watching television (depending on what you watch), but become problems when they are done in excess. Some activities are dangerous and prohibitive in any amount. The problems are acute when they become out of control and interfere with our normal functioning. Romans 6:15-23 speaks of the way in which we become slaves to these things and habits. It may lead to death spiritually and even physically. We must become "slaves" (give ourselves over) to God or be in union with Christ (v. 19b) that we might replace the evil controls over our lives. The church must be a strong advocate for each member, providing support to overcome habits and problems. As sisters and brothers in the faith we should be extraordinarily understanding and helpful for one another.

Of course we start with prayer, Bible study, support groups in and out of the church, and trust in God's help. There are additional aids, which may be helpful; stratagems I learned from writing. My dislike for writing caused me to find motivations to overcome the resistance. Of the following ideas, the first two were immensely helpful in getting me past my distaste for writing.

    a. Trick yourself. Tell yourself you are only going to spend a minute or two looking over what needs to be done, no more than that. Set a short-term goal. Then go a little further by telling yourself you are only going to extend the effort a little. Soon, you are furiously caught up in progress. Even though I was aware I was tricking myself to get back into writing, it always worked. Am I easily fooled, even by my own self-deception, or are other people also able to successfully benefit from the "sneak into it" method?

b. Momentum. "Momentum" is not just an interesting thought. It is real. When you are going strong, don't quit. The physical laws of motion that keep our solar system going, for example, will work on our minds as the psychology of momentum. Things will remain at rest until some force moves them, and they will remain in motion until an outside force slows them down. When we are progressing well, it is harder to stop, *however*, when we take a significant break it is harder to get going again. Momentum is powerful. Battling a bad habit successfully requires momentum.

c. Avoid phony excuses to start the bad habit again. I have a friend who quit smoking for a few months, but started again when a friend's father died and she experienced stress from counseling her friend through the grief. We look for convenient excuses no matter how phony.

d. Don't wait for special occasions. Often we say we will begin our diet or quit our gambling, or the like, on the first of the New Year or on our next birthday. If we are serious, we begin the commitment now. Waiting until that magic anniversary or landmark is nothing less than procrastination and may be signaling us that our struggle won't be successful.

e. Don't let one misstep get you started again. One of the greatest weaknesses in our struggle to get control of our lives is allowing one fall or weak moment to signal failure. We stumble once, smoke one cigarette or eat three donuts, and use it as an excuse to give up the project. Instead, let that momentary setback make you angry and more determined to be disciplined.

f. Substitute your energies. Verse 19 of Romans 6 suggests that we find new outlets for our energies such as substituting chewing gum for overeating or smoking. Romans suggests we invest our time in Christ, serving God and others. Commitment to such activity and ministry will divert our thoughts and actions from those that have been defeating us — something to the order of, "idle hands are the devil's tools"?

W-7. Have You Hugged Your God Today?

Purpose Statement: *What does it mean to love God and do we?*

Some of the great Psalms (19, 23, 33, 96, 104, 145, 148, 150) that praise God in glorious fashion describe an enthusiasm for God that isn't heard as often any more. We need to reread these Psalms and ask ourselves if they express our feelings of devotion and faith. And if they don't, does it disturb us?
   a. Why don't we love God? Of course, we love God. Then why is it we aren't reading some of these exuberant Psalms with eagerness and joy? Two possibilities come to mind. First, God is abstract and we find it difficult to love the invisible and mysterious. Second, we seldom feel the need to love God — or, at least, make any changes in our relationship with God at this time. Considering the first suggestion that God is abstract, we find it so much easier to love our family and friends because they are physical and more visible. It seems easier to experience their love for us. God's love seems indirect and remote. While we do see and feel the results of God's love: life, joy, beauty, satisfaction, forgiveness, and so much more; it is not easy to make the connection with the abstract. We look at the beautiful and special things of life and say they are gifts from God, but we don't see God directly. This leads us to the second suggestion that we feel we are getting along nicely without God's help. We "earn" everything we need and want, and for most of us, it comes too easily. Consequently, a comfortable and materialistic lifestyle isn't conducive to sensing the need for God. We would be surprised to know how few Christians find time, or even the desire, to worship God every day.

b. How do we go about loving God? Stopping taking God for granted is a good start. Reading these Psalms with the desire to capture the feeling and attitudes of those who originally recited them in special worship moments, and asking why they felt such adoration for God are ways to experience God's love. Continually reminding ourselves the love, beauty, and joy we experience each day is a part of God's gifts to us, will cause us to associate our appreciation with God. Loving God is a very real and warm gratitude within. It continues in thankful service as we use our time, energies, talents, possessions, and environment as loving stewards to express our worship of God. Loving God is being more loving of other people. We have to want to experience the exhilaration expressed by those who recited these Psalms as acts of love for God.

W-8. Religion That Will Scare You To Death

Purpose Statement: *Is there still fear associated with some religion and should there be?*

Some sermons may still be using fear and possibly even threats to jar listeners out of complacency. By direct chiding or indirect suggestion, some folks in the pew may be led to believe they are terrible "sinners in the hands of an angry God." Concepts of burning hell and eternal torture are alive and well in some of our churches. Some of us may be trying inadvertently to frighten people into a rebirth experience or into accepting Jesus. And, we find scriptural support for scaring church members straight; for example, Acts 5:1-11 relates the incident where Ananias and Sapphira are struck down, presumably by God, for not turning over *all* of their property to the church, and then lying about it. It seems excessively harsh. Another example from the Old Testament claims God wants people who work on the Sabbath to be put to death (Exodus 31:14-15; Numbers 15:32-36). Few of us would be ready to say either of these examples are God's will or God's doing. Yet, we cannot ignore the questions they raise, or the theology of fear that permeates some of our religious beliefs. Perhaps at least three thoughts could be considered:

    a. Should we fear God? After Ananias and Sapphira died, we are told the whole church, was terrified, as were others who heard of the incident (v. 11). Who wouldn't be? Part of our problem may stem from the fact that we mistake the idea of reverence and awe for fear, and we believe that the proper posture toward God is fear. Reverence or awe is not fear, but respect and wonder. Fear is for things or people that are dangerous or threatening. God is neither dangerous nor threatening if we are to believe Jesus. Reverence is for what is good and wonderful.

    b. Is God's love different from ours? When we speak of a loving God, the kind Jesus revealed to us, and 1 John 4:7-21 described (v. 18 even tells us that there is no fear in God's love), some say God's love is different. We are told God is so great we are unable to understand love at that level, and what seems to us to be a cruel act or a ridiculous law, is not so in God's eyes. Hogwash! God's love is comprehensible. It is not different, only greater. Our love is a part of God's love. When we say we do not understand God's love, we mean that God's love for us is so great it is hard for us to believe God loves us that much. But it is still our kind of love — kind, gentle, forgiving, encouraging, affectionate — just to a greater degree. Jesus explained this in Matthew 7:9-11, as well as many other passages.

    c. Why is it in the Bible? Did God really strike Ananias and Sapphira down? Was it God's will that people be killed for working on the Sabbath? Some will say if it is in the Bible, it must be so. What is true about these passages is the people *believed* these things about God. It doesn't mean this is what God was *actually* like, or that God wanted those things to happen. People in Bible days didn't always understand God, like some Christians today. There is ample evidence for these misunderstandings concerning God throughout the scriptures. Two additional questions are necessary to consider.

1. How can we then know what is true of God and what are erroneous beliefs about God? The answer is to measure or evaluate everything with what is consistent with the love revealed in Jesus' life and ministry.
2. Is it possible that God had a different will for people then than now, or God was different in Old Testament times than God was in New Testament times? No, God does not change. Our ideas about God change just as they did over the many centuries in which the Bible was written.

Mistaken beliefs concerning God existed then as they do now. Unfortunately, there are pastors using these frightening ideas in sermons, and Christians who believe them.

W-9. Drive-Thru-Window Church

Purpose Statement: *For some churches and for some church members, a quick and convenient Sunday morning worship service sounds good.*

We shudder whenever we hear that special phrase, "Let's get it over with." Imagine how God feels when he hears one of us saying those magic words in connection with the Sunday morning worship service. Do some of us take a fast food approach to worship? What does that say concerning its meaning for us? Nehemiah brought the people back from exile, rebuilt the city of Jerusalem, and reinstituted meaningful worship in the temple again. The latter part of chapter 10 of Nehemiah describes how important the worship was to the people and their relationship to God. Nehemiah stresses how important keeping the Sabbath was (ch. 13:14-22), and the great lengths they went to to prohibit work on the Sabbath. Psalm 100 speaks of how excited we should be to worship God. In Psalm 84, the psalmist sings about how wonderful it is to be worshiping in church (the temple). It would be so nice even to live there (vv. 3-4); one day at church is better than a thousand elsewhere (v. 10). Contrast that attitude with the attitude of many Christians today who dread going to church.

    a. Is going to church something "to get over with"? Over the years "going to church" has dwindled from an experience that lasted all day, and included Wednesday night services if not more, down to only one hour or less in the morning. Before air conditioning, some churches moved their morning service from eleven o'clock to eight o'clock during the summer months to avoid the excessive heat. After they installed air conditioning, they decided to keep the early morning time in order that church members could "have more of the rest of the day for themselves." Some churches have Saturday night service or mid-week service that may be used as a substitute for attending on Sunday mornings, "freeing up" the whole day. Many of us want church to be convenient, fast, and hassle free. We thought all those people out playing golf on Sundays were Jews or Seventh Day Adventists and were surprised there were so many of them. What are the reasons we don't look forward to going to church?

    b. Do we view it as "doing our duty"? Sunday morning worship has deteriorated to a chore for many of us. It is something we have to do — something similar in appeal to taking our turn doing the dishes. For some, it even may have evolved to become a sort of punishment inflicted by God for our sinful ways, or something God mischievously uses to make our lives inconvenient. It is like exercise: We know it is good for us (although we may not be able to articulate how), but we hate to do it. It is one of the requirements God expects of a Christian. So, what went wrong?

    c. Have we lost any of the real reasons for going? Essentially, we may have forgotten the reason for "church." It should be where we seek God's presence. It is where we find loving fellowship, understanding, and support from sisters and brothers in Christ. It is a time to celebrate our joy, to seek forgiveness, and to receive encouragement, hope, and inspiration. It will be where we acquire knowledge of God's will to help us manage our moral decisions. It is the most important way we can be in mission with others as we share together in a ministry to our world. Suddenly the church service seems all too brief, doesn't it? *Doesn't it?*

W-10. Life's Most Pressing Question

Purpose Statement: *From all that Jesus said, it may be that nothing is as important as how we treat each other.*

Some will identify our most pressing question as how we find salvation. Others will say it will concern how a good God could allow pain and evil in the world. Still others will want to know about life after death. Let's consider an argument for the subject of "how we treat one another" as our most important concern. Human or personal relationships may be of greater value than anything else. We could challenge that idea by suggesting our relationship with God takes precedence. However, we should remind ourselves that Jesus said loving God and loving our neighbor as ourselves are inseparably connected (Matthew 22:34-40). Matthew 25:31-41 has Jesus reinforcing this concept. If we don't love others, we essentially really don't love God. If we love God, we love others.

Consequently, in a world filled with wars, hunger, injustice, crime, domestic abuse, and broken homes, the most pressing or important question becomes, "Am I my brother and sister's keeper?" (Genesis 4:1-9). The answer is quite clear: "Yes!" It only remains to elaborate.

    a. Life is all about personal relationships. We need each other to be whole persons. This includes marriage, family, friendships, and relationships with strangers. Studies reveal babies who were not picked up and loved were stunted mentally and spiritually. Living in isolation is devastating to personality. Nothing is meaningful or fully satisfying unless it can be shared with others. It is always with eager anticipation that I look forward to sharing the events in my life with my family and friends. Life is all about sharing and loving relationships.

b. We live to help others. So much of the teachings of Jesus centers on serving other people. On the other hand, we live in a society that conditions us to make self-gratification centrally important. If personal relationships are meant to be placed first, it is no wonder obsession with material possessions and selfish interests causes social problems. It is inevitable.

c. We must learn to accept love from others. This is not as easy as it would seem. We hear it is better to give than to receive, but it often takes greater grace to receive than to give. A vital part of life is allowing ourselves to be served in healthy ways by our sisters and brothers.

Relevant scripture passages might include the following: Matthew 25:31-40; Matthew 19:16-21; Luke 10:25-37.

X.

X-1. Why Hasn't Jesus Offended You?

Purpose Statement: *Do we understand and agree with all of Jesus' teachings?*

How could anyone possibly want to see Jesus killed? He did only good, revealed God's will, brought the good news, and healed and cared for people. It was a select group — the religious leaders of his day — that clamored for his death, and no doubt it was they who incited the crowd to ask for his crucifixion (Luke 19:45-48; 22:2; 23:18-23).

    a. Why he offended them (for an expanded discussion of this point see sermon Y-9, "What Did He Do That Was So Bad?"). Jesus, by unmasking the hypocrisy of the religious leaders of his day, discredited their authority, sincerity, and dedication to the truth and goodness. He threatened the Jewish Law and seemed to undermine its accuracy. In the fifth chapter of Matthew, he quotes the Old Testament Law several times and clearly changes its meaning. Finally he claimed religious supremacy for himself. To accept the role of Messiah or the relationship with God he claimed was blasphemy. And, to make their case with Roman authorities, the Jews accused Jesus of saying they didn't need to pay their taxes to Rome (Luke 23:1-5).

    b. Why he should offend us. While there may be parallels between how Jesus upset the religious leaders of his day and how he might offend us, there are additional reasons why Jesus would disturb us today. While the priests, Pharisees, and the like felt their livelihood threatened, Jesus may upset our whole lifestyle. He challenges us to give more of our time and possessions away, to take perceived risks (such as giving up our arms and the use of violent force), to shed harmful lifestyles (harmful to ourselves and others), to accept some tasks that are not enjoyable, and to literally change who we are. Knowing this makes us uncomfortable and frightened, instead of angry as the people of Jesus' day became. Being more sophisticated today, we would not try to execute Jesus. Our method of choice is to ignore or misinterpret his teachings.

c. Why hasn't he offended us? One reason we might give for not being offended is that we say we agree with and accept all that Jesus taught. Possibly the real reason we are not offended is that many of us choose to ignore or misunderstand Jesus. If we don't like what we think Jesus might be saying, the easiest ways of dealing with it is to either pretend it doesn't exist and skip over those passages, or interpret the ideas to say something else less objectionable. If Jesus thinks we should not be so materialistic, we excuse our extravagance by saying we are not really rich, just middle income. We need to have a nest egg for security. We don't really have enough for ourselves yet, but when we are wealthier we will give more. If Jesus thinks that physical force and violence is wrong, we interpret it to mean with regard to our next-door neighbor or a family member, and not intended to include other nations. After all those folks are not only enemies, but enemies are also not quite human. They are deranged and can never be trusted.

There is no place for negotiation since they wouldn't respond to reason, love, or peaceful gestures. Or, perhaps, the safest way to deal with potentially uncomfortable teachings of Jesus is to not read or think about those portions of our Bible. If we feel threatened or challenged with certain ideas of Jesus, we should at least be honest and simply say, "I am not ready for that kind of commitment yet. I am still struggling with those issues."

X-2. If It Isn't In The Bible, It Should Be

Purpose Statement: *We need a method of drawing answers from scripture to address a wide variety of issues, subjects that do not appear to be directly discussed in our Bible.*

John 21:25 tells us that there are many other things Jesus said and did, that time and space prohibited from being preserved in scripture; they would fill many more books. We are probably eager to know what some of those subjects would be. Were there some critical teachings that would be extremely helpful to have — teachings that would answer many of our questions and speak to our needs today? Because we believe that the Christian faith is relevant to all of life, the minister today must be prepared to preach on a great variety of current and important issues. Does the Bible always help?

    a. The Bible doesn't deal specifically with many issues. One of the difficulties of preaching is that there are many subjects that do not seem to be covered in our Bible. Since there weren't very many cars in biblical times, if we choose to preach on the topic, "Christians and safe driving," we must settle for very general or generic scriptures that speak about "caring for others" or "loving your neighbors." It is much like preaching on the "perfect" prayer that Jesus taught us (Matthew 6:9-13) and wanting to say something about "thanks as an integral part of a prayer." While it isn't specifically mentioned in The Lord's Prayer, it certainly would be implied. One of the dangers in following a liturgical formula for preaching such as the lectionary is the possibility of missing critical topics not dealt directly with in any specific scriptures. As responsible and astute pastors we, of course, work those issues into our sermons one way or another. Occasionally, we struggle finding Bible material that can be used directly with subjects we need to preach about.

    b. Some examples. Some of the subjects we might feel compelled to examine as Christians that may not be directly mentioned in our Bible could include the topics in the following list among many others: Christians should appreciate this wonderful world. We want to know more about eternal life that is not so cryptic and dramatically exaggerated. How do we deal with the gap between science and religion? Why does the world seem so cruel at times? It would be helpful if our Bible said more concerning racism, making mistakes, "shunning" naughty people, or befriending and witnessing to them, or how to conquer bad habits. What is the purpose of the world and life? How do we really distinguish real "good fruit" from phony behavior? How important is intelligence for our faith? A more thorough discussion concerning sexual ethics would be helpful. Why are there so many denominations? Is gambling wrong, and why? What is, and what is not, appropriate for social activist behavior and protesting? Certainly, we would want clarification concerning the Bible's definitive position on such topics as going to war or capital punishment.

c. And yet, the Bible does give counsel. The secret to finding answers for our questions is to appropriate a comprehensive understanding of what generally constitutes a Christian lifestyle. It means developing attitudes and sensitivity instead of finding and memorizing simple individual verses we may quote regarding a specific topic such as, "Jesus said we shouldn't make fun of people." This means in order to receive the maximum help from our Bibles, we must engage in an in-depth study of Jesus, his life and teachings, to develop an understanding of the Christian way of life. Such concentrated and diligent study causes us to become intuitive in our feelings for what it means to be a Christian. It becomes a lifetime task providing us instinctive sensitivity in all moral and social issues.

X-3. Reasons Not To Go To Church

Purpose Statement: *If we are to be evangelists and help others find a meaningful life within our church family, it is imperative to know the reasons why others may not be interested in "church."*

Mainline Protestants are concerned about the drop in membership in their churches (note sermon V-1, " 'Feel Good' Religion: A Contemporary Theology"). We are all concerned when church members stay away from church or are apathetic about their church affiliation. If the churches are to deal with this serious problem, we must know why people don't go to church and what we can do about it. The reasons may be many, but here are at least four important ones we might hear.

   a. "Church isn't relevant." The church has a checkered history, and yet has been an instrument for enormous good in society. Historically, we owe the Christian church for the beginnings of medical, educational, and most other social programs in our society. The subtle and overt moral influence the church has wielded in our society through the ages is immeasurable and powerful. The question, "What have you done for me, lately?" could be asked of the church. To the question, "Is the church still making a significant impact on today's world?" the answer is, "No." At least, the impact is not what it has been in the past during those moments when the church was at its best, and it certainly is not as significant as it needs to be and could be. Some of our churches spend their energies preaching the "feel good" religion that some Christians want to hear, since it doesn't inconvenience us. What is needed is a message directed to the urgent and poorly met needs of our communities.

   b. "Church doesn't really help me." If the church is failing to meet community concerns, it also may not be speaking to our personal problems. Does attending church or having an active life in a church really make any difference in our lives? Some seem to be getting along without the church in their lives, while others with problems don't see how the church could help them. Although this is an erroneous assessment of what the church can do for us, it is an honest opinion of many unchurched persons. First, those who think they are doing fine without the church, aren't. Second, for those who recognize their needs and believe the church doesn't have the answers, we have the challenge of introducing them to the real church.

c. "Sermons are boring." Not in this church, of course. But if you ever find yourself a member in another church somewhere, sometime, remember that preaching is a responsibility of the entire congregation. You need to be in conversation with the minister concerning the topics for sermons. Let the pastor know what your questions, concerns, and needs are. Be in dialogue with the pastor analyzing each sermon with positive and challenging responses. Make the pastor relevant and exciting.

d. "Church cuts into my free time." However we may react to such a statement, it seems to be a common feeling among many. We have only so many hours left over after work and whatever other activities we give priority to. Going to church will bite into our golf, movie, party, nap, hobby, television, or other vital activity time. We must convince others that the church matters.

Scriptures might include the story of those reluctant to follow Jesus (Luke 9:57-62), John's letters to the seven churches (Revelation 2 and 3), and Amos' message to the people (4 and 5).

X-4. Religion In A Disposable Culture

Purpose Statement: *Has the over-indulgent nature of our rich and abundant culture carried over into our church life?*

Disposable cameras, contact lenses, cups, plates, plastic eating utensils, razors, diapers, and spouses seem to have been the order of the day for some time now. The fact that we may be responsible in recycling habits does not ameliorate the damaging mindset arising from using something once and discarding it. Apart from the senseless waste involved, there is a nagging feeling of the lack of attachment or meaning to things. Has it become passé to appreciate things and feel grateful for our abundant life and the convenience we enjoy? Is the sole value for anything wrapped up in what it will do for our immediate gratification, knowing we will soon have bigger and better things to throw away? Is our attitude one of believing everything exists for our good times and the heck with the environment, aesthetics, or anyone else? Prophets constantly had to remind the people of the Bible of what God had done for them. When Moses led the Israelites from Egypt and out of slavery, they soon began to grumble and complain (Exodus 17:1-4). Despite all God did for them, they quickly began to worship a new deity (Exodus 32:1-10) in the golden bull, essentially saying to God, "What have you done for us, lately?" Out with the old God and in with the new. Is there a residual of the *disposable* mentality in our church life? I think so.

    a. Sunday morning worship seems expendable. It is easy to miss a Sunday or more. It is always there any time we can make it. The reasons why some people miss church can be amusing, and of course, there are legitimate occasions for absence such as illness, emergencies, football on television, sleeping late, and similar crises. For many people, Sunday morning worship is for when there is nothing else happening at that hour. Unfortunately, we don't often appreciate how much our presence at church means to others in the church family, let alone what it does for us to be worshiping in a community of faith. Jesus was regular in his attendance at church (Luke 4:16), but then he may have needed it more than we do.

    b. The church seems expendable. We can change churches like we change jackets, because we believe one church is like any other. "After all we are all headed for the same place anyway." Granted, a close connection in the Christian family should exist across denominational lines, and no church or denomination has a corner on the truth. But the easy way we play "musical chairs" with churches doesn't represent broadmindedness and tolerance, as much as it represents the lack of attachment we have to a church, either the denomination or a local church. Its tradition and its family of fellowship mean so little. We hardly will acquaint ourselves with what that congregation believes before it may be time to move on again.

    c. The Bible seems expendable. We say we live in a world of gray, nothing is black or white; there are no absolutes. This could loosely translate into the idea that we don't have many guidelines for behavior. "Rules are made to be broken." "Things change so fast, rules are soon outdated." "There are no longer any absolutes." One wonders how relevant we consider the Bible for our lifestyle or our ethical decisions. Like our country's flag, the Bible has been revered to an icon status where it has lost its meaning and significant purpose. We idolize it. We don't read it.

X-5. Too Heavenly Minded To Be Any Earthly Good

Purpose Statement: *Is it possible to be too religious?*

Do others recognize us as Christians? Do we recognize others whom we believe are Christians? Do we recognize them as Christians because they have told us they were, because they go to church, or because their actions clearly reveal their faith? There are various postures Christians take that reflect their faith. Perhaps we shouldn't be judging others in this respect, however, it is important that we do some self-examination. How do we come across to others? Four possibilities, among many, come to mind.

    a. The pious. One of the dictionary definitions for this term is religious activity or posture "springing from actual or pretended religious devotion." More often we tend to identify "pious" in the negative sense: One who is pious poses in a self-righteous manner to impress others for self-aggrandizement. This particular posture distinguishes those who actually believe they are saints, very much like the

Pharisee in the temple (Luke 18:9-14) who seemed assured of his goodness. Is it possible to fool ourselves? Can we adopt the pose long enough to begin to believe it? Some of us feel uncomfortable around the very pious; not uncomfortable in the sense that we know we should be, but aren't, as good as they are; but uncomfortable as in the presence of play-acting or pretentiousness. Some identify the pious as those who use "God talk" in excess. Everything is, "Praise the Lord," or "I'm sure it must be God's will," or "God has a reason for this." Going through the motions of self-righteousness is like wearing an "overzealous costume" that makes it difficult to communicate with the rest of the world.

b. The simple. Either due to limited capabilities or lack of effort, some of us give little serious thought concerning our faith and religious beliefs. We cling to superstitious ideas or foolish doctrine because we don't question their validity or because it would seem sacrilegious to challenge such ideas. Those who belong in this category are vulnerable to the next religious con artist or misguided zealot that comes along. We wonder how otherwise intelligent people can be taken in by some sect, or fall prey to weird beliefs. If it sounds religious we may be foolish enough to think it must be good. Paul warned the Corinthians (11:1-4, 12-15) about following false teaching that sounded good.

c. The phony. These are the Elmer Gantrys. They are the predators who know they are wrong or evil and are using religion for personal gain or entertainment. Surely the religious leaders that Jesus castigated so soundly (Matthew 23:1-36) were divided between the pious and the phony. Thank heavens these characters are few and far between, and yet we need to be on guard that a little bit of each one of us isn't phony.

d. The wholesome. It would be difficult to find any more challenging passage outlining Christian behavior than Romans 12. Verse 3 is particularly appropriate. Our proper posture must be humble service. We must be down-to-earth, real people. Down-to-earth doesn't mean worldly, but having the ability to understand or relate to the world, communicating with others (who may be quite worldly) in a meek, gentle, humble, and concerned way with a genuineness that is wholesome. It is effective because it is a posture others can trust. They will feel secure, understood, and cared for in the presence of such a person.

X-6. Pearly Gates Entrance Exam

Purpose Statement: *What does it take to get into heaven?*

There are a multitude of jokes concerning recently deceased persons meeting Saint Peter at the Pearly Gates hoping to get in. (Did Peter get to be the gatekeeper because Jesus gave Peter the "keys to the kingdom"?) Once three good friends died at the same time. By happenstance each was a member of a different denomination. Peter told them they only had to answer one question correctly to get in. To the Lutheran he asked, "Can you spell *dog*?" The Lutheran responded, "d-o-g." "Correct," said Peter, "You may enter." To the Presbyterian, Peter asked if she could spell *cat*, which she did and she was admitted. The Methodist thought, "How easy this is." He stepped up for his question and Peter said, "Spell *eschatological*." There is a significant emphasis placed on getting into heaven by the Christian faith. Conservative Christians make getting saved prominent in their preaching, the New Testament is concerned with the subject and it is uppermost in the thinking of many Christians. What would it look like using the analogy of college entrance exams?

 a. What would the test be like? Is the test on:
  1. Predestination? Paul seems, on occasion, to think salvation is predestined (Romans 8:29-30) and even used the term (in some translations). Many Christians have long since dismissed any predestination. We believe in our free will, and God's respecting of our freedom to choose good or bad. It would be uncharacteristic of

the God, Jesus revealed to us, to create anyone who did not have a chance for the same eternal life as others have. This can't be the right answer.
2. Works? Everyone says we can never "earn our way" into heaven, as doing good to others for the sake of our own personal salvation is simply selfish. Good works must result from an honest concern or love for others. Even though Revelation 20:12 seems to hint at salvation by works, this is the wrong answer, also.
3. Faith? While Jesus gives greater emphasis to a life of works, Paul stresses salvation by faith as the sole criteria. Then there is the book of James. It is in James 2:14-26 that we find the powerful idea that if faith is real and works are unselfish, they are *absolutely inseparable.*
4. None of the above? As totally indispensable as faith and works are to the Christian, perhaps when it comes to salvation God is far more merciful than we ever give God credit with our beliefs.

b. How is it graded? It could be viewed as more of a "placement" test. Instead of determining if we make it or not, it may be more like "at what level do you enter: freshman, sophomore, junior, or senior?" Instead of *either/or*, it could be a matter of *where* — where on the spiritual plane we enter heaven. To change our analogy, it may be like taking our religious temperature. Our spiritual life may be warm or cool or any degree in between. Our spiritual status may dictate the placement of our soul in heaven. We enter eternal life at the level of our faith maturity. Everyone makes it, it is simply a matter of where you come on board and start your spiritual journey in the new spiritual world. This has the merit of God's never losing a single soul in defeat, and certainly synchronizes perfectly with God's ultimate love.

c. How do we prepare for it? Clues from the teachings of Jesus indicate that we actually don't prepare; at least in the sense of "trying to get to heaven" or living in such a way as to be sure we will be saved. "If we seek to save our life, we lose it" (Matthew 10:39). We do serve for the sake of serving and for the sake of others. The great judgment (Matthew 25:31-46) is a wonderful parable where the "saved" seemed to not have been aware of the process. They just simply loved and served with abandonment and were surprised later to be told of their salvation. Their intentions didn't seem to be to get to heaven or save themselves. They didn't let their "right hand know what the left was doing." They were not self-conscious about their faith or their works. The message of Jesus seems to be to love and serve others because you know you should and don't worry about heaven.

X-7. Can Compassion Be Turned On Like A Faucet?

Purpose Statement: *How do we get motivated to actually love others?*

The question intrigues me and is perhaps one of the hardest to answer just as was the question asked by the sermon Q-10, "Pink Bunny Batteries," "How do I remain enthusiastic about my faith?" Jesus admonished us to love others as we love ourselves and to even love our enemies (Matthew 5:44). Paul tells us to love our enemies (Romans 12:20). Much of 1 John is concerned with loving others (1 John 2:7-11; 3:11-18; 4:7-21; 5:1-5). We know what to do in a general way: love others, but how will we be motivated to do it? Certainly, if we care enough to ask the question itself, this is a big step in the right direction. Can we make ourselves love someone? Three things we might think about would include the following.
- a. Definition. We need to know what love is, the kind the Bible talks about.
    1. It is intellectual rather than emotional. This is not to say there aren't any emotions involved, as there will be deliberate feeling and caring; however, it is a love for others (strangers or enemies) made as an intellectual commitment or decision. We will have sincere sentiments for others.

2. It is service, good deeds, and intentions. This means it doesn't have to be personal. We may never meet many of the people we love by donating money for charity, praying for them, donating blood, or volunteering through a service-oriented organization. It is vital and beautiful even when it seems mechanical in nature because we do the right thing when no personal relationships are involved. In contrast, romantic love apparently is a natural and unintentional response. We may not choose to love a certain person in this way, it happens. The love Jesus spoke of is more decisive and intentional, and later becomes natural.

b. Motivation. Are there three ways to be motivated to love:
   1. God gets us going,
   2. another person stimulates us, or
   3. we exercise a willful decision?

No doubt God is busy all the time trying to motivate us to love each other, *but we must respond,* as God never violates our free will. We may be more directly influenced by personal experience with others in special need. But, usually it is left to us to initiate acts of kindness. If we are experiencing God's love in a meaningful life of faith, our compassion for others will result. Yet there still may be times when it must be a cold decision, "How can I love that stranger?" Knowing it is God's will and the right thing, we need to "just do it."

c. Illustrations. It helps to remind ourselves of the inspiring stories of others who showed love in beautiful ways. We have heard stories of compassion, for example, a couple that adopted and loved the boy who killed their child in a car accident. We read about the person who jumps into the river to save a stranger or goes into a burning building to rescue someone. Such acts of Christian love, and myriads of other examples, will motivate us to be compassionate children of God.

X-8. I Embarrassed God Again Yesterday

Purpose Statement: *Each day we find a variety of ways to offend God and others and must be reminded to be constantly on our guard.*

God was embarrassed for me today as I did things that disappointed God, even though I will be forgiven. Remember Paul's famous confession in Romans 7:14-25? He said he did what he shouldn't do and didn't do what he should do. By suggesting this is human nature, he implies you and I are guilty of the same shortcomings. There are things we do wrong out of ignorance, but in this instance Paul may be concerned with those times when we are aware of the inappropriateness of our thoughts and behavior. It is a matter of not having self-control. The sins of Bible leaders such as Paul and Peter can never become excuses for our improper thoughts and actions. One thing we can anticipate each day is that somewhere along the way we will stumble and need to say, "I did it again, God, I'm sorry."

    a.   I entertained impure thoughts — did you? Remember the collective national gasp when President Carter said that he "lusted in his heart" on occasions? Such thoughts will occur: try not to think of the word "hippopotamus" in the next two minutes. Our world throws temptations at us causing us to entertain "those kinds of thoughts." The question is, "How entertaining?" The critical difference is, "Are such thoughts just fleeting and momentary and quickly dismissed, or are they pondered to the point that we would act upon them if we had opportunity and knew we would not get caught?"

    b.   I disliked someone — did you? We know God wants us to love everyone and treat everyone fairly and without prejudice. However, at one time or another haven't we all been guilty of unfavorably judging someone on her or his looks after brief meeting? We know it is wrong, and our sin may be compounded if we allow that negative judgment to influence the way we will treat or relate to that person.

c. I had selfish thoughts — did you? We are told self-preservation is a natural instinct in creation. Jesus also tells us that we are not animals and do not live by instinct. There may be occasions when we will be called to lay down our lives for another. At least, we must love our neighbor as ourselves. Christianity calls us away from selfish feelings and actions, however difficult this may be.
d. I acted inappropriately in front of others — did you? How many sermons have we heard on the subject of our responsibility to be a Christian witness to those around us? What we say and do is a great influence on others and especially critical because we are known as Christians, which brings added responsibility to be on our best behavior. Even with our imperfections we are capable of acting like a Christian. Try it — you'll surprise yourself.

The solution: (By the way, your pastor didn't really do those things; it was only a trick to get you to confess.) In verses 24 and 25 of the above passage, Paul gives us the secret of self-control. On our own we won't do very well. Paul reminds us that when we seriously desire God's help we are capable of loving deliberations and behavior.

X-9. Why In The World Is There A World?

Purpose Statement: *The subject concerns the reason for our existence.*

This message deals with more of a philosophical question, "Why were we created?"; whereas P-1, "What Is The Point Of Living?" is a practical message concerning what we should be doing. They overlap and relate to each other.

We can only make some educated guesses in an attempt to answer this question. It makes us dizzy to contemplate the mysteries of existence and the universe. As we meditate, it occurs to us that the universe should not exist (except that God wills a universe), and yet it seems as if the universe cannot not exist. Our minds cannot conceive of there being nothing. Of course, God is more than just a convenient answer to a mystery we cannot solve; however, this is our best explanation to the existence of our universe — God wanted it. God loves us and wants us to become people who experience life, consciousness, or awareness. The alternative is nothingness. Genesis 1:24-31 and 2:18-24 tell us that God "was pleased" with creation and thought it "good" to make persons. Consequently, the answers to our question are:

    a. We need a world for us to exist. The generally accepted idea is that a physical world is convenient in order to give birth to souls, which ultimately inherit spiritual bodies (1 Corinthians 15:35-44). It is difficult to find an adequate analogy since whatever we use is physical and not spiritual. It is often compared to a seed needing the soil to germinate and grow. So our bodies provide the necessary house for our spirits as they mature and prepare for eternal spiritual existence, which is the Easter message.

    b. Then what of those persons who die early? If a person dies before being born or soon after, how can their spirit mature without a body to provide the "house" or nurture? The answer must be that God can mature a spirit or soul without a body, but having a long healthy life is a plus or icing on the cake.

    c. Our existence itself is the evidence of God's love. God wanted us to have awareness, to know, to grow, and to enjoy (see message P-1 as mentioned above) life. The famous lines,

> *To be, or not to be; that is the question: ...*
> *... To die, to sleep —*
> *No more ...*
> *(what) flesh is heir to ...*
> *For in that sleep of death what dreams may come*
> *When we have shuffled off this mortal coil*
> *Must give us pause. ...*
> *But that the dread of something after death,*
> *The undiscovered country from whose bourn*
> *No traveller returns, puzzles the will, ...*
>   — Shakespeare, *Hamlet*, act 3, scene 1

seem to be wrestling with the same issues. The Christian's answer is that God knew best and out of love granted us existence rather than the alternative of nothingness.

X-10. Should You Be Sophisticated Or Naive?

Purpose Statement: *What should our natural stance be in relationship to the world?*

How does a Christian relate to the world in everyday activities and relationships? Should we be known as wise, street-smart, sophisticated, and cool? Or should we appear naive, innocent, pure, and generally bewildered by the evil in the world? Once in a while there pops up a literary character who seems to be very good (Christian?) and at the same time extremely naive. Some of us may have this image for the ideal Christian. She or he should be so good and pure that they are unable to comprehend the evil world about them. We might conjure up the vision of a very elderly saintly grandmotherly type being confronted by violent images and the consequent shock she would experience. Such an image is portrayed by Prince Myshkin in Dostoevsky's novel, *The Idiot*, and to a lesser extent Dmitri in Dostoevsky's, *The Brothers Karamazov*, and Prince Nekhludov in Tolstoy's, *Resurrection*. Some critics have said Myshkin is a Christ figure (see sermon V-3, "Could Uncle Tom Be A Christ Figure?"). However, is Christ to be understood as simple and naive in his goodness?

Juxtapose two interesting scriptures that deal with this subject: In Matthew 10:16 Jesus tells his followers (us) to be wise as serpents and innocent (RSV and New English Bible translations) as doves because we are out among wolves. In Matthew 18:3 he then tells us we must become like little children before we can expect to enter the kingdom of heaven. This passage continues on to explain that the childlike characteristic is humility.

Are sophistication and naivete opposites? If so can they be entertained simultaneously in our person? I think Jesus thought so, and if he did, it sounds good to me.

a. Sophistication. I interpret this to mean very sensitive or aware concerning our entire environment. We need to be knowledgeable concerning the wicked ways of our world in order to protect ourselves and fight against the powers of evil. We cannot leave ourselves vulnerable to con artists and religious charlatans because we fail to understand the ways of the slick, tricky world. Jesus said we would be amongst wolves and could get eaten if we were not clever and aware of the dangers. Gullibility is not a Christian virtue. We need "street smarts," without which we may fall prey to scams that will take our life savings or we may be seduced by phony religious leaders pulling us into superstitious cults. Without knowing the ways of the world we cannot operate efficiently as disciples for Christ struggling against injustice.
b. Naivete. The Christian's version is perhaps better labeled, "innocence." We must be (as much as is possible) humble, pure, innocent, principled, saintly, and persons of impeccable integrity. We may be familiar with all kinds of evil that disappoints and saddens us, but does not shock us. My wife and I were attending a community banquet for the inauguration of a service club. We were sitting at the head table — and, consequently, in full view of the entire audience — I noticed my wife laughing at the speaker who had commenced to tell some off-color jokes. I leaned over and whispered to her that she couldn't be seen enjoying that kind of humor in front of a large crowd that included some of our church members (not to suggest she could laugh at other times). She replied that she wasn't laughing at the stories the speaker told. "I don't understand them," she replied, "I'm laughing at the stern, scowling face you are wearing." We can never give the appearance of doing wrong, but must always look innocent (because hopefully, we are innocent). As Christians, we have the task of witnessing for wholesomeness, the good and the right, while being very knowledgeable of everything that is going on around us.

Y.

Y-1. What If Your Minister Misleads You?

Purpose Statement: *How do we recognize the truth or know we can trust the sermons we hear since we can never know everything perfectly?*

Within Christianity alone, there are a great many brands and flavors. Most churches or denominations make a point of proclaiming biblical truth and God's will. Yet they disagree on numerous issues, even issues of serious contradiction. The only logical conclusion to postulate is that not every one is right. We may even have a sneaky suspicion that all of them are wrong on some doctrines or ideas since we do not have a perfect understanding. Jesus warned us against false prophets (Matthew 24:4, 5, 24). Not every one who claims to be Christian or even called by God to the ministry will know the whole of God's truth and nothing but the truth (see sermon A-1, "Shaking Wolves Out Of Cherry Trees"). Paul also warns us there are false teachers claiming to be able to speak God's truth (2 Corinthians 11:12-15). Are we being misled at times and how will we know?

    a. No one has a corner on the truth. Contrary to what some churches and preachers say, we are all still struggling to find the answers. There are theological issues, social problems, and just plain facts that we find difficult knowing for sure what to believe. For example: churches disagree on whether one needs to be baptized to be saved. Each of us should be wary of those who claim to be the true church with the unadulterated gospel.

    b. Ultimately, we are the final say. As much as we would like someone to tell us the right doctrine in order that we might memorize it and never have to think again, it can't be done. It is up to us to sort through the debris and confusion for a sound set of principles and theology that serves us. As Paul said, we must work out our salvation and faith, he could have added, "theology" (Philippians 2:12). We must find the beliefs that answer our questions, give us assurance, and provide moral direction. It becomes our own personal struggle. Recognizing that no one church has all "the truth," we choose which church best fits our own individual beliefs and spiritual needs.

c. Challenge everything. We must question and challenge (take with a grain of salt) everything. No matter how impressive the authority may be, we should never blindly accept what we read or hear, but examine it for validity, looking for inconsistencies and errors. The most respectable pastor could be wrong.

d. Run an authenticity test. Ask some salient and practical questions. Does the idea or belief appeal to our selfish interest, or can we find substance and meaning in it despite the fact we may not like it, or despite the fact that it may make us uncomfortable? Second, does it hurt anyone — others or ourselves? Third, are we hearing or reading this with an open mind or are we stuck on some prejudice or biases? Fourth, is it consistent and reasonable?

e. Let Jesus arbitrate it. Finally, we must add one more critical test. Is the doctrine or theology consistent with the life and teachings of Jesus?

Y-2. Will Sports Craziness Infiltrate The Church?

Purpose Statement: *Will the fanaticism we see in spectators at sporting events ever become a part of our church life?*

It may seem too far removed — the sports world from the church — for there to be any relationship between the two. Yet, it seems legitimate to ask how much some of our cultural mores, values, behavior, idiosyncrasies, and lifestyles will affect our church life. That would include sporting events. After all, it is the same crowd that haunts the stadium that frequents the chapel, or at least there is some overlap. It can be distressing to think our church members are in the stands with their shirts off and bodies and faces painted, screaming with their fingers in the air. Their performance is especially inspiring when they notice the camera panning them. What if the values and conduct displayed at the ball game contribute to their expectations in church? This inquiry should include other cultural elements: for instance, how the disposable mentality affects the church (see sermon X-4, "Religion In A Disposable Society") and what relationship our superhero phenomenon will have for our faith (see sermon Y-3, "Batman, Wonder Woman, And Other Superheroes"). Sports fans' behavior may be becoming more bizarre in its enthusiasm. Even the staid game of golf is attracting obnoxious fans. Soccer fans have been known to stampede each other to death.

Some of these sports fans appeared in Jerusalem around the year 30 A.D. After a large crowd enthusiastically greeted Jesus as he entered the city, Luke 23:13-25 tells us later in the week the crowd (were any of them a part of the Palm Sunday crowd?) cried, "Crucify him and release the murderer, Barabbas." Some of our Friday night fight fans were at the cross mocking Jesus. What lies behind such behavior and how does that enter into our religious situation?

    a. We need to identify with a winner. Our egos are very fragile and need stroking. Some of us suffer from a low self-esteem. We question our worth and adequacy, wondering if our lives are successful enough. Sublimation can take the form of identifying with a winner, which may be a sports team. Our identification can become very intense and produce the unseemly behavior at games that embarrasses us. When our team wins, we win. When our team loses, we lose. If we don't think we have enough going for ourselves, a loss by our team can be hard to endure. While the Sunday morning crowd may not be the same crowd that attended Saturday's game, a few of us in church could use some bolstering from time to time, and be reminded that God loves us. Showing love to one another is unbelievably nurturing and healing, and we don't need to identify with a winner because we are all winners.

b. We like to have a common enemy (opponent). An athletic team may have a great *esprit de corps*. Fans may experience team spirit. Some disposable youth may find community of some sorts within gangs. Nations rally around a war effort. A common denominator is having an opponent or protagonist with which to struggle. Such an archrival or an unpopular opponent unites us in spirit as a team against the foe in another "we" versus "them" scenario. It extends from a friendly rivalry to a tragic level where we attack another nation. We all want to be a part of a team effort, working together to achieve a goal, win a prize, or destroy evil. Unfortunately at times, this takes on the nature of a patriotic frenzy to destroy others of God's children that we have labeled an enemy after dehumanizing them. The church and Christians must be careful that other "lost" people or "misguided" churches don't become a common opponent. Our team spirit or fellowship must be united in a wholesome version of community. Our common foe will be evil, injustice, poverty, hate, war, and distortion of truth. Ours is the positive reconciling, caring, peacemaking teamwork that is mutually inclusive.

Y-3. Batman, Wonder Woman, Jesus, And Other Superheroes

Purpose Statement: *How is Jesus like, and not like, our superheroes?*

Our culture has created the superhero world of Superman, Captain Marvel, Supergirl, Batman, Robin, and many others. The heyday of these comic characters may stem from a more economically depressed time and reflect our society's desire for miracles or some agent to bring relief — or I could be wrong. It may simply be nothing else but one form of entertainment in the world of comics. We still like the idea of a hero riding in on a warhorse and rescuing us from the bad guys. It is no different from any adventure novel or movie where we want the good to triumph and the evil to be destroyed or at least punished. There is no question but that the people in Jesus' day were looking for a superhero in a Messiah, and some believed Jesus filled that role. He was greeted on Palm Sunday with great expectations. Is there any more that we can glean from this subject theologically and what it might mean for us?

    a. What Jesus had in common with other superheroes. Like Superman, Jesus helped others, had special superhuman powers, fought for justice, and was that someone very special we could look up to. The stories of walking on water, exploits with miraculously filled fishnets, stilling storms, and healing all kinds of illness qualify him for the superhero category. Even if he didn't do all these things, the stories that persist indicate the expectations the people had and the reputation he developed. We can trust Captain Marvel, Batman, and Jesus to rescue us.

    b. How he distanced himself from them. There are conflicting thoughts in our gospels concerning Jesus' attitude toward identification with the Messiah. While there are certainly instances where he seemed to accept the role, there are many more where he clearly put down his superhero status and/or activity. He refused to defend himself when arrested in the garden. He declined the superpower available to him to "bring in the kingdom," or to get down from the cross after the crowd mocked him with, "Save yourself" (Matthew 27:39-43). When asked to perform miracles he decried such display (Matthew 12:38-39). There was so much injustice and evil where Jesus might have used super normal power to destroy it. Captain Marvel would have.

    c. How he was different from our superheroes. I am not very conversant with all the Batman, Robin, and Wonder Woman literature, but I doubt very much they were ever heard to say, "Love your enemies." Matthew 5:38-48 records teachings of Jesus that no superhero would ever utter. Turn the other cheek; go the second mile; do good to your enemies. If Superman suggested such ideas, that issue of his comic would probably be his last. He would have to look for a new career. Can you hear Captain America recommending the Beatitudes? And yet, when the crowd urged Jesus

to come down from the cross to prove his power, it was his great love reflected in his prayer, "Father, forgive them," that convinced the soldier in charge who Jesus really was (Luke 23:34-47). In Matthew (27:54) the officer pronounces Jesus the Son of God. Jesus stands alone when he says to love our enemies.
   d. What does this mean for us? In our worst moments we want our enemies to be destroyed. A Rambo or James Bond is the kind of hero that satisfies our sense of justice. Jesus brings an entirely new philosophy of peace and kindness that says enemies are children of God, also.

Y-4. How Do You Define Yourself?

Purpose Statement: *Who are we and what do we let determine who we are?*

As we know, there are different images of who we are. There is who we think we really are, who we want others to think we are, whom we should be at our best, who others think we are that we may not be aware of ourselves, and so forth. The question we need to ask ourselves is, "Who do I think I am and what do I want others to know about me?" Many sermons have been done on the question Jesus asks Peter in Mark 8:27-38 (v. 29 in particular), "Who do you say I am?" Most of those sermons deal with Peter's answer that Jesus was the Messiah. The question that should logically follow would be concerning who we think we are. What are the criteria we use to define ourselves? In most cases the answer is integrally tied to other persons and what we want them to think of us. Thus, in a sense, we often let others define who we are. Here are some possibilities:
   a. Appearance. It is not uncommon for each of us to place an inordinate emphasis on what we look like (see Y-10, "Don't I Look Nice?"). We are not satisfied with just looking clean and neat; we must have the proper dress with clothes that are in style. The fashion industry dictates the acceptable

trends we must wear to be like others. "What is current fashion?" may not be quite as critical as it used to be, but has not gone away. Latest accessories include body piercing and tattoos, which are also statements about who we are. The image we desire to convey is paramount to how good we feel about ourselves. "How do I define myself? Just notice how I look. It may be obviously superficial, nevertheless, this is me."

b. Family. Occasionally, our history is important to us and we take pride in our nationality or our family. This is another superficial attempt to impress others, yet, if we come from a family that has been particularly successful or is well known, we may wish to flout our connections. Wealth is another popular indicator connected with family. Ethnic identification may work either way, negatively, as well as positively, depending on particular prejudices.

c. Interests. This is one defining moment for me: when someone becomes acquainted with my particular interests, or when I discover the interests or hobbies of another person. I get excited when I can share my special interests with some unwary person. Some of us could talk all day about one of our hobbies or pastimes. And I am always asking other people about the things that interest them or what their hobbies may be. We may partially define other people by what interests them.

d. Personality. Perhaps, this comes closer to who we really are. We should be conscious and cautious concerning the possibility of acting sincere or phony in our attempt to impress others as we define ourselves.

e. Occupation or profession.

f. Relationship to Jesus. Are we as interested in defining ourselves by our faith as we are by the alternatives mentioned above? The pressing question should be, "Do we define ourselves as Christians?" This doesn't mean in the sense of being a member of the majority, popular, or dominant religion, but in the sense that Jesus speaks about in the rest of the Mark passage cited above: taking up our cross or committing our life to our faith. We may not envision defining ourselves for others as a follower of Jesus as much as we should. This doesn't mean by constantly telling everyone, "I'm a Christian." It means by how we act and treat others as a result of our constant awareness of who we are as Christians. Are we cognizant throughout each day that we made a commitment to follow Jesus?

Y-5. Everything I Needed To Know I Learned In Sunday School

Purpose Statement: *Is it possible that Sunday school is more important than public school education?*

Many members of the churches I served were in the field of education and many more contacts with the teaching profession came through my wife, who was an educator. Most of these people would disagree with the thesis of this sermon that what we learn in Sunday school is of more value than what we learn in our public school education, including college and graduate school. In making comparisons, we first note that public education involves learning facts and knowledge about reading, math, history, science, and an unbelievable variety of subjects that help us get along in society and find employment. Undeniably, this is all extremely valuable. However, I am suggesting the subject matter or content of the Sunday school experience is of greater value. (Many educators prefer "church school" rather than Sunday school education, thereby eliminating the notion that it only happens on Sundays and cannot continue during the week. This is a good idea.) What is it concerning Sunday school curriculum that makes it more important than public school?

    a. Right and wrong. The thesis of this message is that if one had to choose between two alternatives: being well-educated (in reading, writing, history, and other subjects) and being a moral person, the latter is preferable. To state it simply: It is better to be a good person than a smart person. A person who knows right from wrong, who is

honest, loving, kind, sensitive, and all those good things is more preferable than the person who has mastered many secular facts and knowledge.
b. Personal relationships. The church is also about personal relationships. Our world, at least much of our own country, is well educated. Yet, we are unable to live together peacefully and lovingly. War is constant. Social problems seem insurmountable. Families are dysfunctional and in disarray. Crime and preventable hunger and poverty are excessive. But we are well educated. What is wrong with this picture? The church provides the solution, but is not being utilized to build better communities.
c. Nature of God. Having a healthy theology and understanding the nature of God is imperative if we are to appreciate our lives, others, and our environment. To not know God is to be partial or incomplete. No matter how much we know about reading and writing, without God there is a void or emptiness. It can lead to depression, dissatisfaction, despair, and other personal problems, as well as social problems.

There are four additional things that need to be clarified.
a. Public education is extremely important; it is vital. I am not denigrating it in any way, but wholeheartedly endorse it.
b. Public education may actually achieve many of the goals that Sunday school attempts in terms of morality and personal relationships. And, to the extent any education is an exploration of God's world, it deals indirectly with the nature of God.
c. Fortunately, the two types of education are not mutually exclusive. They are both necessary and doable side by side.
d. While Sunday school education is so critical, it is also true it doesn't always live up to its potential. At times it will fail miserably. It depends on volunteers and sometimes people who are not well versed in the curriculum. Attendance is not mandatory, and unfortunately can be sporadic. Sunday school is so very valuable, and it is necessary that we give it greater attention.

Y-6. So You Think You Got Away With It

Purpose Statement: *Sin hurts us even when we are unaware of its consequences.*

Our sense of justice cries out for sin or wrongdoing to be punished (mostly in others; it's nice if we can get away with it). We may become angry when someone who breaks the law goes unpunished. Some people have a strong desire to see someone who has committed a particularly heinous murder be executed. What would our position have been if we were part of the crowd who brought the woman to Jesus to be stoned to death? Would we have approved or been pleased when Jesus arranged for her commutation (John 8:1-11), or would we have cried with righteous indignation, "That's not fair!" since, according to Jewish Law, she should have been put to death. Do we think that David deserved greater punishment than he received in the murder and the adulterous affair with Bathsheba (2 Samuel 11)? Does it often seem the guilty or those deserving punishment escape their deserts, or do they? Our concern is not about consequences after we die: heaven or hell and whatever justice awaits us there. What about justice now? Do some cruel and selfish persons seem to live happy and rewarded lives, while good people suffer unfairly? Remember the story Jesus told about the selfish rich man who wouldn't help the poor man (Luke 16:19-31)? Although he suffered in an after life, do we think he deserved punishment in this life? He didn't seem to experience any bad consequence before he died. Are there occasions when we get away with sin in the here and now?

    a. Invisible punishment. The insidious nature of consequences or repercussions is they may ramify in a very quiet and unperceived way. There are diseases where the symptoms are sneaky and hidden, and we only become aware of them when it is too late or sometimes not at all. Sin and consequences may be operating the same way. We may think we got away without any repercussions after doing something wrong. To use smoking as an analogy, a smoker may have a long period of time where she or he feels no ill effects from the habit, and all the while the foreign substance in the lungs is taking a serious health toll. Many of our sins may seem to be totally without reverberations. Lies we told haven't been discovered and we haven't suffered. Opportunities to help others that we ignored didn't seem to hurt us (Matthew 25:41-46). However, the insidious nature of sin is that it quietly eats away at our soul, or spirit, undetected. It tarnishes our integrity, dulls our sensitivity, dissolves our moral judgment, and diminishes our very being without our awareness. And, just like the drinker who is less able to appreciate the effect of alcohol on his or her senses after each succeeding drink, sin can destroy our personhood. The spiritual law of cause and effect is at work. Put a warning label on your doorpost saying, "You will get caught." Shakespeare wrote in *King Lear*, Act 1, "Time shall unfold what plighted cunning hides, Who covers faults, at last shame them derides."

b. Inadmissible awareness. There is a strange phenomenon whereby we know the truth but won't admit it. In our best moments, when pushed into a corner, we will admit certain things are bad for us and it is wrong to do them. However, the defense mechanism of our choice is to not think about it. Like Scarlet O'Hara, we won't deal with it today. We know speeding is wrong, but it hasn't hurt us, yet. We know we shouldn't gamble. We're aware we should be more involved in community service and church ministry. However, our sins of commission or omission haven't hurt us, yet. Or have they?

c. Unadvisable ignorance. To feign ignorance, or actually be oblivious to what sin does to us is devastating. This sermon is our wake-up call, and after hearing it we can no longer plead ignorance. Because we have heard this sermon there will be another repercussion to our sins: a troubled conscience with which to deal.

Y-7. Do Circumstances Ever Justify A Sin?

Purpose Statement: *It is time to discuss situation ethics.*

Everyone tells us the world is not black and white. Instead of clearly defined options and obvious answers, we have extensive areas of gray where we flounder for moral direction. Situation ethics enters the picture right about here. Situation ethics may have had its moment in the spotlight during the '50s and '60s, but because of the nature of the issue it is timeless, and it is a theological conundrum.

One scripture that introduces the subject as well as any other would be the account of Jesus and his disciples walking through the grain fields on a Sabbath. His disciples picked wheat and ate it, which constituted work according to the legalists (Matthew 12:1-6). The Pharisees confronted Jesus with the charge that his disciples were breaking the law concerning work on the Sabbath. Jesus replied with a reference to a historical incident preserved in 1 Samuel 21:1-6 concerning David and his soldiers who, though they were ritually unclean, went into the temple and ate the holy bread. Jesus said this was against the law (v. 4). This was a "situation ethics" moment.

    a. What is it? In some instances, situation ethics will be the "lesser of two evils" in decision-making. It is the "one size doesn't fit all" of morality. This means we create rules of right and wrong to govern our conduct, such as: don't steal, don't kill, and don't lie, only to find they may need to be suspended given certain circumstances. People of the social ethics persuasion tell us that we cannot have blanket rules to cover every contingency. For instance, we agree stealing is wrong, but when it becomes a matter of life and death it is permissible to steal food to save a life. This may have been what Jesus was saying concerning David's unlawful eating of sacred bread in the temple. We should obey the rules unless there is some unique reason why that rule should not apply. That is situation ethics. Should we consider it bending the rules or exercising the fine print?

b. Is it necessary? It is true that special circumstances may call for doing what would ordinarily be called a sin. A very simple example I always use is the hypothetical hospital room where a patient who has had a heart attack and is in critical condition inquires about her family. By hypothetical coincidence her family has just been killed in an automobile crash. If the nurse or doctor tells the patient the truth it may be too much for her weak heart and kill her. Knowing she will eventually recover and be able to receive tragic news, they tell her her family is doing fine. They lie. But isn't it better to lie (a minor sin) than to kill the patient (a greater offense)? Another less dramatic example from scripture would be Jesus' excusing the woman of the accusation of foolish waste when she poured expensive perfume over him (John 12:1-8). Ordinarily, the disciples would have been right. Jesus, no doubt, would agree it might have been better to sell the perfume and use the proceeds for the poor. However, he chose to ignore the economic good deed in favor of making her feel she had done something very worthwhile instead of embarrassing her. If we are to do the very best thing in every situation, we must weigh all the elements involved and do that which is the least harmful. It may mean committing a "sin" to avoid committing a greater sin. Often a circumstance will inadvertently pit one principle against another principle. The dilemma forces us to make a decision that will violate one principle in order that we might observe another, and we must choose the "lesser of two evils." For example, do we protect the freedom of speech even if it harms someone by violating her or his right to be free from abuse?

c. Are there dangers? If we are ever going to exercise the privilege of justifying some "sinful" conduct by claiming situation ethics dictated a certain action even if it seemed questionable, we should acquaint ourselves with the pitfalls involved. I once identified a dozen or more, however, let's mention only three.

1. Too often we believe our situation is unique and different from what others experience, and it calls for action that will be inappropriate for others. Has our biased subjective judgment excused behavior that was not appropriate? Are we, indeed, really the exception to the rule others need to follow?
2. Examples of situation ethics too often overlook third, fourth, or even more possibilities. The tendency is to only see two options. To take a favorite example from one situation ethic expert: should a women give herself sexually to a man who is having problems of emotional sexual anxiety and seduce him in order to "help" him over his impotence? The situation ethicist may say, "Yes, we should break the rules for a higher good." What ever happened to other alternatives? Why not explore seeing a therapist?
3. Another danger is in making the end justify the means. Is it a sin if it works? This is a mistake we make in international relationships. We justify killing innocent men, women, and children in war to protect our interests. (This sermon idea only begins to explore the issue.)

Y-8. Goldilocks And The Three Bears Problem

Purpose Statement: *So many situations call for finding the "happy medium" or the delicate balance between too little and too much.*

In the Sermon on the Mount, Jesus speaks about the Christian life being likened to a narrow gate or road (Matthew 7:13-14). A fair interpretation is to say he means it is difficult, and not easy, to find. Or, having found it, it will be difficult to traverse. One of the complications is that oftentimes our behavior goes too far to one side or the other. Using an analogy of driving a golf ball down the fairway: by going too far left or right we will be in the rough, or worse. It is much like a highwire or tightrope-walking act, where it is necessary that we stay on the line. I was struck with the comparison between this scripture idea and the Goldilocks story. Goldilocks was confronted with the problem (beside the possibility of being eaten by bears) of finding the most comfortable bed and a porridge that was neither too hot nor too cold. Very often the need arises to find "the golden mean" or the fine balance between the excessive and the insufficient. The proper stance or posture in ethical behavior is usually a narrow middle ground.

This should not be confused with the related problem that uses similar positioning. In this case (converse, if the idea in the previous paragraph can be thought of as convex) "middle of the road" is sometimes a bad thing and to be avoided. We shouldn't straddle the fence. Instead, we should take a position or a stand on one side or the other. We must have the courage to express our convictions. Revelation 3:15 tells us we should be either "hot or cold" and not lukewarm. (But that is another sermon, F-10, "What Are You Doing Out Of Jail?" perhaps.) How does the Christian deal with the Goldilocks problem?

    a. Examples. The importance of this sermon results from the numerous possibilities of situations where it is possible to have too much or do too much, or not do enough. When it comes to pride, too much is arrogance and too little is self-depreciation or low self-esteem. With our faith, we can become overly exuberant and zealous, or at the other extreme have no passion or enthusiasm. In terms of generosity, we may be either extravagant and give too much away, or become miserly and stingy. When it comes to self-discipline, we can be overly rigid and restricting, or have no self-control. Consider the necessity of finding the balance between a workaholic and a lazybones. The list appears endless as many virtues, attitudes, or actions lend themselves to the possibility of too little or too much. How do we find that happy medium or golden mean?

    b. Solution. The first step would be simple awareness. Knowing the possible dangers, and being cognizant of the phenomenon in each situation is critical. Next, we may learn and grow as we test limits of appropriate behavior through discussion and dialog with other Christians in Sunday school and other groups. A critical criteria is asking what the results will be if we move a little farther to the left or right. Will it be harmful to others or ourselves in any possible way? While there are certainly other possible guidelines, an important one would be to ask, "What would be the most Christlike?"

There seem to be so many instances where it is necessary to find that narrow gate or fine line making this issue a major Christian concern.

Y-9. What Did He Do That Was So Bad?

Purpose Statement: *Why did anyone want to kill Jesus?*

The idea that anyone would want to kill Jesus is preposterous. He did only good things. Think how he healed people, bringing them immense relief from suffering and inconvenience; how he was concerned for the poor and unfortunate; how he was always kind and loving. Crowds often would gather around him making it difficult for him to find time to eat or rest. On one occasion, he had to get out in a boat away from shore because they pressed about him. He almost had to sneak away to get a break. They loved him. Certainly no one would want to hurt such a good person, the one we call the Son of God. It is true the local Roman authorities were worried, that with his popularity, he might instigate a Jewish uprising against Rome. In such a case, Rome might replace the local government representatives who failed to squelch such a revolt. This would give the Roman leaders motive for getting rid of Jesus. But that is another story. Instigation for his death came from the Jewish religious leaders, and we should consider the things he actually did that disturbed them enough to provoke such violence.

    a. He discredited the religious leaders. Reread his castigation of the religious leaders in Matthew 23:1-28. He denounces their corruption, their hypocrisy, and their ignorance in the harshest of language. Pharisees were the respected authorities of Jesus' day and his condemnation of their leadership knocked them off their pedestals. Many of them must have been sympathetic with the Pharisees because of their long tradition in the religious law and their "special connection" with God. Their position and very livelihood was threatened. Imagine how clergy today would react to a personal attack on their authority and position if they were exposed as Elmer Gantrys or similar to some of the fallen television evangelists.

b. He undermined the religious law. Jesus not only broke Jewish Law, but also said things that would seem to weaken its authority, such things as: "The sabbath and law were made for people; people were not made for the sabbath and law." He and his followers did things — "harvested grain" and healed on the sabbath — that was disrespectful of Jewish Law, culture, and tradition. When you undermine trust in the sacred, you are meddling with people's faith. Consider the history of translations of our Bible. New translations, such as the Revised Standard Version in the '40s and '50s, constituted blasphemy for many and created significant anger. When historic criticism suggests parts of our Bible are myth, and some passages contradict other passages, the response may be scathing. Knowing this, it seems reasonable the people would be upset when Jesus quotes the Old Testament Law several times (Matthew 5) and proceeds to suggest changes. He was dangerous to their faith.

c. He claimed religious supremacy. Of course, such a claim would give credence to everything he said and did. He accepted identification with the Messiah, which would have been considered blasphemy in his day and warranted his death.

d. Would we be offended? Would similar attacks on our religious institutions and traditions go unrequited? Could we tolerate criticisms of our Bible quietly? Anyone making the claims about himself or herself today that Jesus made, would be considered a charlatan. Any accompanying miracles would be considered phony magic tricks. Yes, we would be offended or disturbed. While, hopefully, we have matured as a society beyond the point where we would harm the messenger, we do not always accept criticism and new truth gracefully. With the help of biblical study, much prayer, and using our imagination, the church needs to consider the unpleasant truths that Jesus might have for us today. It could only be for our good, but would we, too, become angry?

Y-10. Don't I Look Nice?

Purpose Statement: *Our obsession with physical appearance does not fit with Christian values.*

Some talented author (that would be me) has written a book about physical appearance (and other related issues) titled, *Frankenstein and Miss America: Who's Who and Who's Not.* It describes what happens when we give too much attention and place inordinate value on how we and others look. It permeates our entire society in many different ways, from kids picking on peers, to Miss America pageants that glamorize certain people as the ideal, to how we want our loved ones to appear in the casket. Excessive emphasis on appearance determines who gets which jobs and who marries whom. Wouldn't we all agree this is contrary to Christian values and harmful for all of us? While Matthew 6:28-30 is speaking about the dangers of placing too much importance on possessions, it would not be a stretch to recognize in it a warning concerning our preoccupation with what we wear and how we look. The comparison between King Solomon all decked out and the simple natural beauty of a wildflower is a poetic treasure of truth. For each of us, the real beauty is who we are and the uniqueness each one of us brings to the table. Our personal uniqueness is to be appreciated, not denigrated by revering the glamorous beauty queens while pitying or shunning the "ugly" ones among us. (Physical appearance is one of the concerns in Song of Songs 7:1-9.)

    a. We create a world of false values. Someone once described our world as a display window where a prankster had gotten in and changed all the price tags around to send the message that inexpensive items cost more and high price items were ridiculously underpriced. This may be an apt analogy of the phony world with twisted values we have created. Money and success become more important than love and family. We have allowed physical appearance to become one of our most popular values despite its superficial nature. It could be said we are more concerned with how we appear — what we wear, our makeup, body ornaments, and the like — than the kind of person we will be. Greed, commercialism, comparative wealth, and communities that tempt us with immediate selfish gratification, all have corrupted our value systems. A central theme in the teachings of Jesus is proper priorities and a "first things first" philosophy.

    b. It becomes a terrible waste. It is easy to see how we spend our money and energies going off in the wrong directions trying to meet society's artificial standards. Think of what we spend on fashions, makeup, body ornaments, and by extension, other accessories such as cars and houses to create an image of who we would like to be. Think of the eating disorders and diet efforts (although certain diet schedules are necessary for health) we suffer through to become more attractive to others. I am told the Academy Awards and similar events have become a parade of outrageous fashion in efforts to appear in the most stunning costumes and hairdos. Is there really anyone who honestly cannot see the dramatic contrast between this and the modesty of the Christian lifestyle?

    c. Note what it does to others. By idolizing certain "beautiful" people, we are telling others this is what we all aspire to become. This is the ideal you should measure your worth by. To the extent you may not measure up, you are somewhat defective. There are those in our society who do not feel good about their appearance. Some may even be ashamed of how they look. This is the result of our false standards and obsession with appearance. It not only hurts the person whom society (you and I) has singled out as not attractive and perhaps even ugly; it also doesn't do the "chosen" and attractive person any favors either, although they are usually oblivious to the fact. Christianity, among other ministries, is in the business of making people feel good about themselves, as worthy and loveable individuals. Christianity is not in the business of lifting up counterfeit values.

(G-3, "Beauty Is NOT In The Eye Of The Beholder!" is a related message)

Z.

Z-1. Knock, Knock — Who's There?

Purpose Statement: *How do we handle the religious zealots who knock at our door?*

I was at a ministers' retreat one time when one of our clergy friends came up to our circle of five gathered in idle conversation and singled out "Bill," one of our enthusiastic members, saying to him, "I have a new knock-knock joke. You start it." Bill, eager to enter in, quickly said, "Knock, knock." Our friend replied, "Who's there?" to which Bill obviously had no reply. He had been had, and we all laughed. Though taken in, Bill looked around the room for someone on which he could pull the same stunt. He rushed over to another informal group of five as I tagged along saying to myself, "Oh, this will be good." Bill accosted one of the groups quickly, saying, "I have a new knock-knock joke. Knock, knock." The other person dutifully replied, "Who's there?" Obviously Bill had no reply. He had been had a second time.

What do you say to the enthusiastic religious person who knocks on your door to tell you you are not in the right church until you join their church? They quote scripture better than you can and will not take "No" for an answer. Do you not answer the door? Do you open the door and rudely turn them away? Do you just patiently listen and feebly argue until they get tired and go away?

    a. First, respect them. They may come a-callin' from God. They may have the message all garbled and be unaware of their confusion, but their heart is in the right place. They mean well. They just don't appreciate their narrow intolerant perspective. But you love them anyway, and treat them with respect. Of course, there is a small outside chance they are speaking for God. Remember how God came knocking on Samuel's door (1 Samuel 31-10) and Sam had a difficult time recognizing God. If nothing else, it can be an inadvertent reminder to you to get off your apathy.

But be kind even when they get pushy. I always deal lovingly with telemarketers; some of them really believe in what they are selling. I say quickly and kindly, "Thank you, but I am not interested at this time," and hang up immediately preserving their time so that they might call you.

b. Second, be secure in your faith. If they bewilder you with their scripture and arguments, whose fault is that? Each of us needs to have a working faith; a religion that answers questions and gives us assurance. Paul said for us to work out our faith with fear and trembling (Philippians 2:12); or to be very intentional in knowing our God and God's will for us. Through Bible reading, prayer, church school, and retreats, we should be prepared to match wits with whoever knocks on our door. It is we who should have a message for them. Turn the "knock, knock" around. Once you have worked out your faith, you will be eagerly desiring for someone to knock at your door.

c. Third, ask probing questions. Challenge them with difficult questions: "How does God take care of us?" "If God is loving, why does God allow evil and pain in the world?" "Are some good people lost?" And don't settle for simple non-answers, keep pushing. They won't know it, but you are doing them a favor. Ask yourself the same questions and see if your faith has some intelligible answers.

d. Fourth, don't wait until they knock on your door. This is not about preparation for debate. This is about having a sustaining faith. Some people have lost their faith due to unfortunate incidents they could not handle. Someone's child is killed in a car accident and they don't know why, so they blame God. They surrender their faith because of poor theology. It is more than just believing in God or Jesus. We are told (Luke 12:11-12) that when we are challenged we should not worry because the Holy Spirit will give us the right answers. I think not — unless we have developed a relationship with the Holy Spirit beforehand. Start immediately building a sustaining faith and when you hear the knock, knock, no matter who's there, you can say, "I'm ready!"

Z-2. The Multi-Billion-Dollar Rodent Den

Purpose Statement: *Too many people are missing the intelligent and appropriate response to alcohol use.*

Alcohol is more destructive than all the illegal drugs put together. The amazing thing is we continue to tolerate it, or worse, encourage its use. It is a multi-billion-dollar business with a great deal of power that has deceived a large portion of our population. We are pouring those billions of dollars down a rat hole in terms of the waste and destruction we purchase. Since the drain on our financial resources is gradual, squandered by individuals, it doesn't seem so formidable. As a lump sum, disregarding the destruction it has purchased, that money is enormous in its potential, if turned for good use. One of my friends gives perhaps a too vivid description for beer by saying it ought to be poured back into the horse (don't use that from the pulpit).

Proverbs 23:29-35 is one good description of the use of alcohol and its effects on our bodies and minds. Would you mind answering four questions for me?

   a. Do we really understand how destructive alcohol is? Its devastating nature is beyond belief. Get the latest statistics on alcohol related deaths and injuries on the highways, homes destroyed and families broken, health costs, and non-driving deaths linked to drinking. Just among college students alone, about 1,400 die from alcohol-related accidents each year, and about 70,000 sexual assaults and date rapes are attributed to campus drinking each year (*Time*, April 22, 2002, p. 18). Our media releases information for us in a steady stream. Some recent articles include some of these studies:

      1. There are an estimated 600,000 heroin addicts and 18 million problem drinkers in our country.
      2. More than 5,000 babies are born each year with fetal alcohol syndrome.
      3. A study revealed that workers having ten or more drinks a week away from work have significantly

higher number of injuries on the job as well as a much higher rate of absenteeism.

The list of impressive statistics on alcohol-related destruction is very long.

b. Do we really care about the welfare of others? I keep coming back to Romans 14:13-21 as a significant scripture calling us to responsible Christian living where Paul specifically mentions abstaining from alcohol use (v. 21). If we actually love our sisters and brothers we will refrain from those things that will hurt them. By using alcohol ourselves we not only influence others (including children and youth), but we give our permission for its use, the impression it is not harmful, and support for the industry with our purchases.

c. What is it good for? There are many dangerous things that also serve a good purpose such as cars, I suppose. If something is a necessity, we are willing to pay the price or run the risk involved. But, when something is only pure expendable luxury ("luxury" seems too nice a word here), and is a proven serious harm, why do we tolerate it? The use of alcohol as a social lubricant or personal relaxer makes it a sad and pitiful crutch. Would a farmer buy feed for cows knowing that it would cause a significant percentage to die, get sick, and destroy property without any benefit? If any new drug is suspect, we pull it off the market until it is thoroughly tested.

d. Why don't we do something? Apparently, we are trapped in the notion that fighting the alcohol problem is for old-fashioned, do-gooder, naïve, simple folks — similar to the unfortunate stereotyping we have for the Women's Christian Temperance Union membership. I have the greatest respect for the WCTU and feel their cause is right on. A modern version with a little narrower focus, MADD (Mothers Against Drunk Drivers), is also a significant organization that is right on target. Why doesn't the Christian church act decisively? Many messages could be illustrated by the following story, but it fits nicely at this point:

a little girl listened with rapt attention to a problem dramatically presented from the pulpit only to see everyone walk out of church calmly afterwards with an apparent lack of concern about the sermon. She jumped up and excitedly asked her mother, "Isn't anyone going to do anything?" Her mother replied, "Be still, people will think you are strange." Alcohol use and abuse warrants the same concern we have for traffic accidents, cancer, heart disease, crime, and world hunger. Join MADD, WCTU, or get the local church stirred up. Do we think that prohibition did not work? In fact, it was very effective (see sermon E-10, "Better Moonshine!").

Z-3. Wicked, But Worth It

Purpose Statement: *We need to recognize the delicate balance between the realization we are sinners and at the same time very special and worthy of God's love.*

Jesus was able to relate profound ideas in very poignant ways. One such parable worth reading and rereading for a constant reminder of our humble station and the special love God has for us is the story of the two men in the temple (Luke 18:9-14). The one was proud and thanked God for being such a good person, while the other acknowledged his sin and was very humble. Couple this story with the other teachings of Jesus that reveal our preciousness and God's love for us (prodigal son, lost sheep, lost coin, and others). This should keep us in the narrow path between gross pride on the one hand and poor self-esteem on the other. A Christian appropriately deals with his or her sinfulness. I often tease my wife and say, "You are so wicked." Her answer, with an evil little smile on her face, is, "But I'm worth it." She may not have caught the spirit of this subject, so this sermon is for her edification.
    a. Recognize our wickedness. There are at least five or more kinds of sinners, and each of us is surely one of them.

1. The vicious person who is seemingly devoid of love, but who probably still has some spark of goodness or divine in her or him.
2. The usual run-of-the-mill sinner who may have no significant relationship to a church.
3. The caring unbeliever who is a non-religious person, but is a kind and loving individual.
4. The good church person who has her or his sneaky sinful side.
5. The self-righteous, pious-parading "saint" who wants everyone to know how much better they are than other people.

Which one are you? We should never try to place anyone else in one of these categories, but it would be well for each one of us to identify our place in the list. Confessing our sins in the morning church service — perhaps the only place it happens for some of us — has often become merely a perfunctory prayer. Knowing we will be forgiven should not diminish the discomfort our sins cause us.

b. Recognize our forgiveness. Apparently, forgiveness never happens until we are
   1. truly sorry and repentant.
   2. are sincere in our resolution to change, and
   3. forgiving of others in turn (see sermon S-7, "Get Over It!").

   Remember the unforgiving servant parable (Matthew 18:21-35) that Jesus told.

c. Recognize our worthiness. The difficult part is to be able to maintain some sense of dignity and self-worth if we really experience the seriousness of our sins, how much we offend others at times or the unlovable attitudes we indulge. I'm not sure the tax collector in the temple who Jesus said was "justified" felt his pardon and redemption; I hope so. His remorse seemed excessive, but obviously sincere. Finding the appropriate posture is a narrow threshold between recognizing our sinfulness and our value as children of God.

d. Recognize the dignity of others. Recognizing our own sinfulness should be an excellent beginning as we build relationships with others. As sinners we will be unable to look down on, or judge, others. We won't have a "better than thou" attitude. At the same time we won't excuse or condone unsatisfactory behavior. We will recognize others along with ourselves as fellow sinners on this moral journey together (see sermons Q-1, "Ate With Any Wicked People Lately?" and Q-2, "When Your Friends Are Naughty").

Z-4. Pilgrim Or Tourist?

Purpose Statement: *How serious (or loose) is our connection to Jesus Christ, the church, and Christianity?*

Pilgrim and *tourist* are intriguing words when juxtaposed. "Pilgrim" denotes someone who is on a serious religious journey, usually destined for a holy shrine or event. A "tourist" would be more of a casual sightseer out for enjoyment. If those are adequate descriptions, then which one best identifies our spiritual journey? One of the central events in the final days of Jesus' life was his entry into Jerusalem at the beginning of Holy Week (Matthew 21:1-11 and the other three gospels). It is an exciting event for Jerusalem as the crowd was cheering Jesus as exuberant-like fans at a football game. Where were they later when Jesus was crucified? Were those who greeted him when he entered Jerusalem the same ones who either jeered at him at his execution or watched apathetically? Or were they there only for the celebration and good times when all was glitter and glamour, and gone when things took a more serious turn? I have a friend who said that when she was a child and the circus came to town her family would turn out for the circus parade and sit on the curb watching the clowns and elephants march by. It was free. The family never attended the actual circus because it was too expensive. We can excuse the way they chose to see the circus, but can we excuse our behavior when we engage in the celebratory but not the sacrificial life of the church? Is our relationship with Jesus one of an acquaintance or a member of our family? Is our journey a pilgrimage or a vacation? Let's focus on two questions:

    a. Is our church experience a life-centering event or a social activity? When we examine our relationship with the church, are we able to be objective and honest in evaluating what the church means to us? Do we find our activity and connections with the church family generally casual and not very demanding? Do we "enjoy" the Sunday morning service, or at least tolerate it? Do we attend church dinners, and perhaps even take our turn helping? Do we usher, sing in the choir, attend women's or men's groups, and perhaps even participate in Bible study groups? Would we characterize our activities in the life of the church as comparing favorably to belonging to a country club or lodge? Or can we say our relationship is more serious? We wouldn't miss church unless there was an illness or emergency. We feel that we are followers of Jesus. We make sacrifices for our church family and for the church's ministry in our community and the world. Would we profess our faith in Jesus if it meant losing our jobs, having friends and even family members not understand us, or even cost us our lives?

    b. How real are the teachings of Jesus for us? When we read the teachings of Jesus and come to the hard parts, are we disturbed and challenged, or do we feel totally comfortable and at ease? Jesus spoke of the difficulties his followers would encounter. He mentioned persecutions, making sacrifices, serving others, and witnessing for the faith. He said we must feed the hungry, go into all the world (out among the wolves) serving and being threatened, preaching and healing. Are you and I called to do this? If we are not uncomfortable with these challenges, we may have misunderstood Jesus. If we consider his teachings to be "nice" ideas, we have successfully wrapped them safely up in cellophane and stored them away. Are we pilgrims or tourists?

Z-5. Blemishes And Biblical Authentication

Purpose Statement: *"Defects" or "flaws" in the Bible do not necessarily diminish its value or truth as the word of God, but, strange to say, may even be evidence of attempts of the Bible writers to be accurate and truthful.*

Some may suggest there is no need for further evidence to prove the Bible is the Word of God than its own claim to be God's Word. We only need to accept that doctrine on faith and it will be sufficient. On the other hand, one could argue that it doesn't hurt to have additional supportive testimony. We should welcome all the validation wherever we might find it. For example: it could be suggested that the imperfections and contradictions of the Bible are not negative, nor do they represent weaknesses; but in fact they may be creditable and authenticating. Conservative Christians no doubt worry about any hint of contradictions or "mistakes" in scripture and for good reasons. If it is possible to point out any discrepancies, where then, does one stop? It leads logically to the question, "If we can't believe this statement, what can we believe?" For the conservative it must be all or nothing. Well, that is a problem with which they must deal. In the meantime, we "mainline" types can take solace in the fact that any contradictions or mistakes in our Bible can have a positive spin. Such a possibility tells us that there was no effort to cover up, change, or leave out difficult and contradictory passages. (By itself this does not prove the Bible, of course. However, it speaks for the honesty and carefulness of the writers, not to mention the countless scribes who hand-copied the manuscripts over the centuries, and the translators.) Consider the following strange evidence:
    a. The heroes are not candy-coated. There is never any attempt to cover up or gloss over the defects or sins of the most popular of God's people in the Bible. Their crude mistakes and even horrendous crimes are hung out for all to see. Paul condemns Peter for his racism (Galatians 2:11-14). Abraham offers his wife to Abimelech (Genesis 20:1-11) and Isaac may have been ready to do the

same (Genesis 26:1-11). David kills Bathsheba's husband to steal his wife (2 Samuel 11). The list goes on. It would have been easier (but dishonest) to change the stories or leave them out entirely in order to preserve the respect and honor of these great biblical heroes.

b. Unaccountable events are preserved. There are details in Bible accounts that would normally be omitted from any other literature as too strange or perhaps insignificant to write about. Such simple and unusual details indicate the integrity of the authors. The two following incidents range from the trivial to the tragic. Mark 14:51 relates the account of the follower of Jesus running away naked. Exodus 31:15 and Numbers 15:32-36 claim that one of God's laws is the bizarre notion that people who work on the sabbath should be executed.

c. Parallel stories abound. Different traditions, of what is probably only one and the same story, are maintained. One should wonder at the constant repetition of stories too similar not to be the same actual event. Many of our Bible stories are repeated with different details. The alternative would be that the Bible world was full of coincidental parallel events such as: the feeding of the multitude (5,000 men in Mark 6 and 4,000 in Mark 8; check the other gospels, also), and Jesus being anointed by a strange woman at Simon's house (Mark 14:3-9) and by Mary at Lazarus's home (John 12:1-8). The list is legion. These duplications are probably simply one story remembered by different people and reported in different ways. Again, the integrity is not in the details, but in the honesty of the authors and the "point" of the story.

d. Obvious contradictions exist. If the Bible authors and copiers were worried about having a "pure" and errorless literature they could claim as infallible, they would have eliminated the many contradictions. Two such examples, among very many, would include the death of Saul (1 Samuel 31 and 2 Samuel 1) and the death of Judas (Matthew 27:3-5 and Acts 1:18-19). Another conundrum concerns Jesus riding into Jerusalem on Palm Sunday on one or two donkeys (Matthew 21:1-7 and same story in Mark, Luke, and John).

Z-6. A Dangerous Way To Read Your Bible

Purpose Statement: *Unavoidably and necessarily we must "pick and choose" which passages in our Bible we will believe, and which passages we will ignore.*

Concerning the scripture read this morning (Leviticus 20:9 and 27, and Mark 16:18); do not try this at home. Though the Bible tells us to stone disobedient children and witches to death, and to not be afraid to pick up deadly snakes or drink poison, who of us would accept this as appropriate behavior? The question that immediately springs to mind is, "What should I believe about the Bible?" Does doubting any passage of scripture, call the rest of scripture into question? What can we trust as dependable and true?

a. First, there are errors in the Bible (see the previous sermon, Z-5, "Blemishes And Biblical Authentation," for some of these discrepancies and contradictions). We know that we cannot obey the Bible advice quoted from Leviticus and Mark cited above. Perhaps God did not strike Ananias, Sapphira (Acts 5), and Uzzah (2 Samuel 6) down dead. That would be contrary to the God of love we know and worship. And we might doubt Elisha commanded bears to attack little children (2 Kings 2). Few of us think we are predestined (Romans 8:29) or believe Jesus destroyed a herd of pigs (Luke 8:32-33). There are errors and contradictions. How will this affect the way we read our Bibles?

b. Second, each of us must pick and choose what to believe. A serious dilemma confronts us. At least two alternative solutions are available for the problem of biblical errors. The more conservative Christian will put a twist on the uncomfortable passages by "reading into" the scripture what isn't really there. (Is this what they call taking the Bible literally?) For example, the "evangelical" may say, "The young man who claimed he killed Saul (2 Samuel 1:1-10), which contradicts 1 Samuel 31:1-5, was lying." *However the Bible doesn't say he was lying. You have to "read that into" the account.* More often, the conservative will simply choose to ignore difficult and embarrassing parts. Isn't this tantamount to "picking and choosing" what biblical passages are "useable" and which are best ignored? This is exactly what the more liberal Christian will probably do, also. So, perhaps all of us "pick and choose" regardless of our theological leanings. We conveniently "interpret" ideas such as what selling all that we have and giving it to the poor really means; and perhaps reject the part about women not speaking in church (1 Corinthians 14:34-35). We may not like it or even admit it, but we practice creative selection when it comes to believing and following our Bible's suggestions.

c. The danger is that we will read with prejudice. No one will refute the idea that when we begin to select certain passages as acceptable and others as not applicable, there is a grave danger that we begin to believe only what we want to believe, and ignore or dismiss as inappropriate the parts we find unpalatable. The Bible becomes for us the gospel according to you and me. By this process it is possible (and probable) that we distort, change, and ignore God's Word. The evidence might be the plethora of different churches with widely held beliefs. If this is unavoidable and a dangerous way to read our Bibles, what can we do about it?

d. Finally, we have excellent criteria for "picking and choosing." The secret is the same one that solves many of our theological problems and is mentioned in other sermons. We measure every idea, principle, act attributed to God and even each teaching of Jesus by what is consistent with the total ministry of Jesus and the aggregate nature of his teachings. We immerse ourselves in the spirit of Jesus by reading over and over his life and teachings until we understand his love so well we are able to intuitively sense the truth. (Or we can sit back and let our preacher tell us what to believe. That would be one way for your preacher to earn her or his $500,000 a year salary.)

Z-7. Skeletons In The Church Closet

Purpose Statement: *The Church is not now, and has not in the past, been perfect. We must acknowledge our sinful history, and work with its current limitations, attempting to be the best "Body of Christ" we can be.*

We should never try to cover up the unfortunate history of the church's failings, past or current, just as the Bible doesn't gloss over the sins of the great biblical figures (see sermon Z-5, "Blemishes And Biblical Authentication"). This sermon could begin by sharing some of the sins of the church through the ages such as: torturing people until they conform to church doctrine, converting people to the faith by the sword, burning witches, supporting slavery, and other terrible distortions of the Christian teaching — for it was done in the name of Christ and the church. Jesus did not make any attempt to hide the corruptions of his religious tradition. Matthew 23:1-36 is one of the most amazing incidents of harsh criticism in literature, and it comes from Jesus. He castigates the religious leaders in hard terms, calling them names, and charging them with serious offenses. He brings the "skeletons" out of the closet for all to see, even describing the leaders as being "like tombs full of dead men's bones" (v. 27).

    a. Skeletons from the past. Select any number of historic examples such as those mentioned above to inform church members as to how the church was not always very moral. Cite corruptions in church-state unholy alliances, pronouncements of church leaders, persecution of Jews and other non-Christians, and other scandals. Of course, we do not want to be totally negative even though the purpose of this message is to deal with our failings and sins as the church. It is necessary to share the beautiful moments and mountaintop experiences in our church history. We have been first in leadership regarding medicine, education, civil rights, welfare, and just plain loving service. The church has served and sacrificed well and so have countless individual Christians. Rehearsing the good and bad past is how we learn and grow.

b. Skeletons of the present. The church has grown, but we're still guilty of sins. Thank heaven, hopefully we are well beyond the atrocities of the past. We do have our scandals and embarrassments today, and we need to admit them, or we will never conquer them. If we really love our church, we will not pretend our mistakes and abuses don't exist. Airing them and dealing with them is mandatory. It is because we love our church that we don't transfer our membership, but remain to criticize and work to make our church stronger and truer to the call of Christ.

c. Skeletons in the future. The lessons of the past and present will be critical to understanding our future ministry as the body of Christ. We cannot seek to "preserve" the church in its current mode as if it were a museum. Jesus' remarks concerning losing our life in service for the sake others is applicable to the life of the church, and crucial for our future. Our business is building the kingdom of God: "Thy will be done on earth...." We won't be perfect and we'll continue to make our mistakes well into the future. But God forgives us and uses us despite the new skeletons we create.

Z-8. The Christian And False Besmirchment

Purpose Statement: *Christians should be extraordinarily careful not to judge others on flimsy and inadequate evidence.*

The phrase, "give them the benefit of the doubt," is so important that it should be prominently located in a Christian's arsenal.

How many persons have been falsely accused of something, or unfairly suspected of some unacceptable activity, and had to live with the mistaken association? They may not even be aware of such an unpleasant or unfortunate accusation. It may have happened to you and me.

Jesus certainly had this in mind when he said, "Judge not," (Luke 6:37).

   a. Judgment. Are we careful enough to not judge someone on superficial or unjustified evidence? I once saw what appeared to be a minister I was acquainted with going into an x-rated theatre. I could have been wrong, and as a Christian I must give everyone the benefit of the doubt and assume I was mistaken. Years ago, a friend of mine in school jokingly reached out as if he were going to take some money from the teacher's desk just as she entered the room. He had no intention of taking it and was only playing around. However, she viciously berated him and unjustly called him "sticky fingers" among other things. We can all create a list of inappropriate and false judgments to use as illustrations (see sermon M-7, "You Have The Right To Remain Silent").
   b. Condemnation. Just as insidious as our own mistaken notions is the gossip we hear concerning others that may be only hearsay. When another person shares a condemnation of someone, we must assume that the evidence is not worthy of our consideration and try to kill the accusation.
   c. Exoneration. We must do whatever we can to make sure a person's reputation is cleared of any taintedness when they have been proven innocent. So often, a stigma attaches to a person accused of an offense and clings long after they have been exonerated of the crime or unsavory activity. Christians should not allow a hint of suspicion or association to linger with someone who was falsely accused and do our best to exonerate that person. Despite our best efforts, individuals falsely charged with such incidents as embezzling or child molestation live with

that identification the rest of their lives. It takes concerted effort to clear away those unfortunate associations.
d. Redemption. As Christians, we go even further and love persons whether they are guilty or not. The old adage, "we hate the sin, but love the sinner," hasn't changed. What a person is or does should not affect our relationship or how we will treat that person. Christianity is all about forgiveness, love, and reconciliation, and remember that our sins are forgiven as we forgive others.

Z-9. We Need To Talk

Purpose Statement: *It is necessary for Christians to sit down together and discuss controversial issues or we will never progress toward consensus. This message is to encourage the process and set the stage for forums and discussion groups in the church.*

You know you are in trouble when you hear the ominous phrase, "We need to talk." Your employer may be about to reprimand you, your fiancé could be planning to break up with you, or someone is about to lower the boom. It is time for pastors to tell the congregations, "We need to talk — about the critical social issues that confuse and divide us such as: capital punishment, prayer and Bible reading in the schools, euthanasia, racism, and so forth."

There seems to be two general schools of thought. One is that the church just preaches the love of Jesus and the people are on their own to interpret what that means concerning the social issues confronting them daily. The alternative thought is that the church must deal with the difficult questions providing opportunities for Christians to sit down together and search for answers in the context of fellowship support, prayer, and church resources. History has shown us that the first method doesn't work. Consider how the church's generic preaching on love alone did not satisfactorily resolve slavery, or more recently, make much of an impact on racism. The church must bite the bullet and confront difficult issues.

We are told Quakers have a belief that if Christians sit down together and sincerely desire to find the truth, or God's will, regarding any difficult issue, and if it is done in a loving and prayerful manner, after much discussion and sharing they will be led by God to gravitate toward the truth. How can any of us not believe this? The church cannot afford not to begin these kinds of prayer and discussion groups on the vital social concerns we face. By not doing so we will remain divided and unable to make any serious impact concerning the problem resolution.

Matthew 22:15-40 describes three attempts by the Pharisees and Sadducees to trap Jesus by asking tricky questions concerning thorny subjects. Jesus, in turn, proposed a tough question (vv. 41-45) for them. Following this we are told (v. 46) that no one dared to ask him any questions. It is necessary for us to ask Jesus questions on these very troubling issues — not to trap him, of course, but to ascertain God's will. As a church, we currently are unable to act with harmony and consistency on such concerns as school vouchers, global warming, or how to deal with terrorists. If the church is ever to make an impact on society, we need to talk — seriously.

To do it properly takes several qualifications. Included among them would be:

a. A sincere desire to know God's will.
b. To recognize our current thoughts may be wrong. No one has a corner on the truth.
c. Be open to new and strange arguments.
d. Be loving and tolerant.

Z-10. If You Can't Say Something Nice ...

Purpose Statement: *Constructive criticism is necessary and helpful, and we need to learn how to give it and take it.*

"If you can't say something nice, don't say anything at all," has its place, but it shouldn't discourage valuable criticism that needs to be heard. Criticism can be insulting, hurtful, cruel, and unnecessary when it is the result of anger, jealously, or other improper motive. On the other hand, criticism can be very good when it is given out of concern and provides needed information for growth and progress. Consider four examples of criticism:

   a. Nation. "America, love it or leave it," leaves a bad taste. I even get angry when I read this slogan on a bumper sticker of some self-righteous nationalist. It sounds as if we are being instructed to go along with the patriotic fervor and ask no questions to just blindly follow. If we are going to be critical of our nation, our government policies, and particularly protest one of our wars, we should get out of the country, as we are not wanted. Those who would silence war protesters, for example, and insist everyone fall into line and accept the administration's international policies without question, are the kind of people who gave permission and blind obedience to Hitler. Since our country is at the top of the list, or very near the top, in percentage of population in regards to crime, broken homes, suicide, incarcerated citizens, drug use, domestic abuse, and other social problems, it behooves us all to take a serious critical stance toward our country. If we truly love our nation, we will not overlook our problems. We will critically attack the social ills that plague us. Amos (2:6-8) was harshly critical of the nation. Jeremiah (11:18-21; 26:7-11; 38:4-6; and others) was threatened because he was a war protestor and accused of undermining the war effort of his nation.

   b. Church. Amos (5:21-24) shared God's message concerning disappointment with the "church" of his day. Their religious ceremonies were hollow and without meaning, and the faith had lost its connection with God. In our New Testament, Jesus reserved his harshest criticism for the religious leaders (Matthew 23) and castigated them with an uncharacteristic vehemence. Each pastor and church needs regular report cards on mission and performance.

   c. Others. Hardest of all is to be critical of friends. Paul felt it necessary to reprimand Peter (Galatians 2:11-14) at Antioch for being a racist and acting falsely. We risk loosing friendships by doing what we think is best for our friends. There may be occasions when it would be important for them to know something that hurts. They may resent our efforts and it could cost us our friendship, but hopefully, it would be done with love and in their best interests.

d. Self. Can we accept criticism from friends or others gracefully? Do we do very well at introspection? Occasionally, we will encourage friends or family to evaluate our appearance, performance, or ideas, but find it difficult to accept their assessment when they are honest with us. We may even lose friends because of their suggestions. Generally, this should be a good source of helpful information if we really want to know and grow. But can we survive another's honest judgment? Even more difficult is the ability to do our own self-evaluation with open minds. Will we see what we need to see, but do not want to see?

If abused, criticism can be mean and hurtful. If given in love, and with honesty, it can be helpful, if not necessary, for our well-being.

Bonus Sermons

Bonus-1. Let Me Tell You How To Vote

Purpose Statement: *Should our Christian faith dictate how we should cast our votes? — Yes!*

From a Christian perspective, let me tell you how to mark your ballots when you step into the polling booth. Each of us uses some criteria to make all of our decisions. How we choose to spend our leisure time; how we will eat, play, or live; how we will spend our money; or how we make our daily decisions are all based on our conscious or unconscious beliefs and values. "What do you believe?" should be the criteria for making our political decisions. Obviously, we will use the information we have gathered on the issues or candidates that will be on the ballot. But, what guiding principles will we use to process this information so as to make the proper choices? I will be so bold as to suggest that our Christian beliefs and values should be the guiding light. We must be so conversant with Christian principles that we can make judgments on civic issues and politician's positions in order to make the "right" choices. What are those Christian values and how do they translate into wise voting?

For scripture we might consider Acts 1:21-26 (telling of the way the apostles voted on a replacement for Judas), Romans 14:13-23; 15:1-6 (dealing with the qualities of a Christian person), or Matthew 5:1-12 (which outlines beautifully Christian values and principles). There are so many others that could be used and certain ones will come to mind as you work through this subject.

We should start with some housekeeping rules. First, we must be reminded of our responsibility. A Christian (as should every citizen) needs to vote. This is one of our special rights under a democracy and to abdicate that exercise is to undermine one of our basic freedoms. Second, the church should never suggest we vote for a certain candidate. Better check; but I think the churches could lose their tax exemption by recommending individuals vote for a specific candidate. However, it is permissible to take a position regarding issues. A pastor may recommend a position on legislation pertaining to such matters as speed limits, welfare, gun control, the death penalty, or other issues. Also, there are many occasions when you and I do not have a direct vote because the matter will be decided by senators or representatives in the legislature. We do have an indirect vote and we must exercise it. We may, and should, contact our legislator with our opinions on the various issues. Finally, have you ever heard the old adage, "There are two things we should never talk about — religion and politics"? Why? They are volatile subjects because of their importance; the very reason why we must discuss them. Thus the reason for this sermon on religion and politics.

    a. Christian principles we believe: Let me list just three from among the possibilities of Christian beliefs and values that should govern our decisions.
       1. A Christian thinks of others and is not selfish.
       2. Jesus admonished us to be wary of riches and excessive material possessions.
       3. The Prince of Peace said that those who take up the sword will parish by the sword.

    There are many more Christian beliefs that we could suggest. However, these three (compassion versus selfishness, generosity versus greed, peace versus war) will suffice to illustrate how we might demonstrate our Christian values in the political arena.

    b. Social and political values consistent with Christian principles:
       1. The Good Samaritan parable and many other things Jesus taught us make it clear that we must have a welfare program and a serious social concern reflected in government action. To say we want to "keep government out of our lives" is to believe that, when left to our own unregulated devices we will always do the right thing, does not bear up under the scrutiny of current evidence.

2. Our economic system excessively rewards and favors many entertainment celebrities, sports figures, and business leaders with wealth beyond any reasonable justification. When given the opportunity to curb these excesses, which become sinful in the light of the destitute and starving in our world, we must consider legislation that brings justice.
3. It is difficult to even imagine that God desires that we bomb innocent women, men, and children in an act of war.

Surely, God's way of love and peace can be accomplished through acts of sincere negotiation and generous aid. God, according to Jesus' teachings, wants us to find ways that work and do not involve violence.

c. Examples: The following examples could be used to illustrate how we apply our religious beliefs to political decisions.
   1. I may not want to wear seat belts or bike helmets because I find it inconvenient. However, as a Christian, I should think of what is best for the general public.
   2. I should choose to vote against tax breaks for the people with excessive wealth and support legislation beneficial to the poor.
   3. As a Christian, I must vote against the obsessive war expenditures and pre-emptive strikes against other countries, especially those that have not posed a direct threat to us (as in Iraq).

To follow up with some additional suggestions, while the church cannot recommend candidates, it can remind us to consider ones who espouse appropriate positions on the issues. Related to this idea is the caution that we do not become taken in by candidates who "use" religion, spout phony God talk, or make pious posture a political strategy. It is not always easy to detect the subtle and tricky ways of a crafty politician. Another concern that complicates issues and muddies the waters is a piece of legislation that purports to accomplish good things, but has hidden attachments that negate the benefits. With the complexity of the candidate's positions on many different issues, we must not become a "one issue" voter. We need to determine which candidate comes closest to our Christian beliefs and values on most issues!

One final thought: how competent do we feel on understanding Christian values, and how comfortable are we with them ourselves?

Bonus-2. Oh, One More Thing

Purpose Statement: *A sermon summarizing the overview of Christian theology or the pastor's key concerns in the church's ministry.*

When I was leaving a church, my last sermon was usually an attempt to give a final summary of the fundamental beliefs I tried to incorporate in my preaching or the major issues I wanted to emphasize in my ministry (and consequently the church's ministry to the community). It was a last chance or a "parting shot" to pull together an overview of the important things I had tried to share with, I hope, some success. It was a simple bare-bones total picture or outline of my preaching or ministry emphasis. (I only pose this message as an example of what a pastor might do during her or his final sermon.) Jesus seemed to do this, particularly in the book of John, though none of us intend to place ourselves on his level. Of the last words of Jesus, the ones I find most meaningful, as final instructions, would be his conversation with Peter when he said three times, "Feed my sheep" (John 21:15-17). Was his threefold emphasis an attempt to say, "This is so important I want to say it again and again to make a lasting impression on you?" Given an opportunity my final words to the congregation would be:

    a. God loves us. It would seem one would not need to say the obvious, but that isn't so, because we also hear preachers talk about a God who does very cruel and unreasonable things. Recently, the news carried the story of a church wall falling on some members and killing them. One pastor's response, said with all good intentions to comfort the people, was, "God did this for a reason, and we are just unable to understand the inscrutable ways of God." On occasions, the Christian theology espouses a (g)od we should fear. Some say God assigns people to eternal torture for simply not believing — hardly something any good parent would do. Our God, Jesus revealed, is a loving, forgiving, and *reasonable* God who wants only the very best for us (Matthew 7:9-11). God never brings us harm. God created a world where pain and evil are possible because of our freedom and the necessity for contrasts: you can't have an up without a down.

b. There is no greater revelation than Jesus. I have tried to repeat this ideal throughout my ministry: we must immerse ourselves in the life and teachings of Jesus to such a degree we naturally and intuitively know what God is like and what kind of behavior is appropriate for the Christian. Everything in the Bible, as well as outside it, must be judged by Jesus. To know what the will of God is, and what truth is, our only effective measure is to test it for consistency with his life and teachings. I have tried to read as many sacred writings of other religions as I can, and nothing else is even close to the great teachings of Jesus.

c. Bring good sense to the Bible. Our Bible is the source for understanding Jesus and God's will. However, it contains some ideas that need to be "interpreted" or just simply ignored. For example, Paul's teaching concerning women is outdated. The Old Testament is full of strange laws no longer applicable to us (if in fact they ever were appropriate), and some passages concerning heaven and hell are exaggerations for emphasis. The Christian must focus on Jesus and (as in the point above) measure all else by his teachings.

d. The good news is eternal life. God's forgiveness, the power of God's love, the possibility of a relationship with God through prayer, and much more culminates in the special gift of life which is eternal. God's special gift to us of existence, consciousness, or being that is eternal is the good news. We are an Easter people.

e. Serving is more important than "getting saved." If we weigh the teachings of Jesus, we find a strong emphasis on loving and serving others (the Great Commandment, the final words to Peter noted above, the sheep and goats final judgment story, losing our life in service and not seeking to "save" it, and so much more), in comparison with so little concerned with "getting saved." How can we read the overwhelming amount of material concerning our love and caring for others and not see it as the central concern in the teachings of Jesus?

There is so much more, but this is one person's basic faith.

Subject Or Topic Index

Aesthetics	U-3
Aging	Q-5
Alcohol	Z-2
Appearance	Y-4, Y-10
Appreciation	T-4, U-3, U-10
Balance	Y-8
Beliefs	P-4, P-9, R-5, R-6, T-2, U-7, V-4, X-1, X-2, Y-1, Z-1, Z-6, Z-9, Bonus-2
Benefits	T-9
Bible Interpretation	T-5, U-7, V-10, W-8, X-1, X-2, Z-5, Z-6
Bible Study	T-8, W-1, Z-5, Z-6
Change	R-5, R-6, R-8, Y-9
Churches	P-9
Church History	P-8, Z-7
Commitment	T-9, U-1, U-8, V-6, W-2, X-1, X-4, Z-4
Compartmentalization	S-1
Condemning	Z-8
Congeniality	P-3
Convenience	W-9
Courage	V-3
Creation	W-3
Creativity	S-2
Criticism	Z-10
Crudeness	R-9
Death	T-3
Demonstrations	U-6
Denominations	P-8, P-9, T-2
Depression	S-3
Dialogue	V-9, Z-9
Dignity	P-7
Disasters	R-1

Divisive	P-9
Doctrines	P-4
Dying	T-3
Education	Q-7, Y-5
Efficiency	R-10
Ego	Y-2, Y-4
Elderly	Q-5
Emotions	R-7
Enthusiasm	Q-10, R-7, X-5, Y-2, Z-1
Envy	T-1
Eternal Life	X-6
Ethics	W-5, Y-5, Y-7, Y-8
Evangelism	S-6, Z-1
Evil	S-9, Z-3
Exaggeration	Q-6
Faith	S-8
Family	U-5
Fanatics	T-7, Y-2, Z-1
Fear	W-8
"Feel Good" Religion	V-1
Fellowship	S-6
Forgiveness	S-7, Z-3
Formality	P-7
Fundamentalism	U-7, W-8.
Geography Of Bible Lands	W-1
Giving	U-8
Goals	P-1
God	P-6, R-1, S-10, U-10, V-5, V-7, W-7
God's Will	R-2, S-1, Y-9
Golden Mean	Y-8
Gospel	R-5
Gossip	Z-8
Growing	R-8, V-2, W-2, Z-9
Guilt	U-1, Y-6
Gun Control	P-10

Habits	W-6
Halloween	S-9
Heaven	X-6
Hell	V-10
Heroes	Y-3
Hiding From God	P-6, R-3
Humility	W-4
Image	S-6
Imagination	S-2
Innocence	X-10
Insecurities	U-5
Insurance	S-10, T-9
Jealousy	T-1
Jesus' Teaching Method	Q-6
Judgment	Z-8
Knowledge	S-4, T-8, V-4, W-3, X-10, Y-5, Z-9
Law	Y-9
Learning	R-8, T-8, V-4, Z-9
Life's Purpose	P-1, V-8, W-3, W-10, X-9
Love	V-3, V-7, W-7, W-10, X-7
Loyalty	Z-10
Mistakes	P-5
Morality	W-5, Y-7
Needs	S-6, T-10
Omnipresence	P-6, V-8
Pacifism	Q-9, S-5, V-3
Patriotism	Z-10
Paul	T-5
Peace	S-5

Phoniness	U-9, X-5
Piety	X-5
Politics	Bonus-1
Practical Religion	S-1
Preaching	V-9, Y-1
Pride	W-4
Priorities	R-10, U-8
Privilege	U-4
Progress	V-2
Promises	U-1
Protection	T-9
Protests	U-6
Punishment	V-10, Y-6
Purpose For Life	P-1, V-8, W-3, W-10, X-9
Racism	U-2
Relationships	P-3, Q-1, Q-2, S-6, W-10, X-7, Y-4
Relevance	X-3, X-4
Religions, Other	T-2
Renewal	P-10, R-3, R-7, V-2, W-2, X-3, X-4, Z-4
Responsibility	R-4, S-4
Reverence	V-5
Routine	V-2
Rumors	Z-8
Safety	P-5, Q-3
Salvation	X-6
Science	W-5
Secularism	S-9
Segregation	U-2
Self-control	W-6
Self-esteem	W-4, Z-3
Self-interest	Q-8
Sensitivity	T-4, U-3, U-10
Sermons	V-9, X-4
Serving	P-2, R-4, T-3, U-8, V-1, V-6, Z-4
Shunning	Q-1

Sin	X-8, Y-6, Y-7, Z-3, Z-7
Sinners	Q-1, Q-2
Social Issues	Q-8, S-1, U-6, V-1, Z-9
Sophistication	X-10
Stewardship	R-10, T-3, U-8
Strangeness	T-7
Strength	S-8
Sunday School	Q-7, T-8, Y-5
Supernatural	Y-3
Theology	V-8, Y-1, Z-1, Bonus-2
Tolerance	T-2
Tragedy	R-1
Truth	Z-5
Values	Y-10
Violence	R-2, T-6
Voting	Bonus-1
Vulgarity	R-9, V-5
War	Q-9
Witnessing	U-6, U-9, V-6, X-8, Z-1
Worship	P-7, Q-4, W-7, W-9
Youth	U-5

www.ingramcontent.com/pod-product-compliance
Lightning Source LLC
Chambersburg PA
CBHW070548160426
43199CB00014B/2422